THE HAZEL-ATLAS GLASS

IDENTIFICATION
AND
VALUE GUIDE

GENE

AND

CATHY

FLORENCE

COLLECTOR BOOKS
A Division of Schroeder Publishing Co., Inc.

Front cover: Florentine No. 1 plate – pg. 160, $12.00; States souvenir tumblers, New York, pg. 61, $6.00 – 8.00; Hazel-Atlas canning jar, pg. 69, $5.00 – 8.00; Criss Cross fired green ¼ lb. butter dish, pg. 102, $60.00 – 65.00; Fancy Ships cocktail shaker, Ritz blue, pg. 15, $70.00 – 80.00; Pink Elephant ice tub, 44 oz., pg. 21, $45.00 – 55.00; Cloverleaf footed candy dish, pg. 153, $70.00; Dots refrigerator jars, pg. 117, $35.00 – 40.00; Concentric Rings orange/tomato jar & tumblers, pg. 36, Juice bottle, $15.00 – 18.00; tumblers, $4.00 – 5.00; Batter jar, waffle, pg. 99, $30.00 – 35.00; Ivy mixing bowl set, pg. 112, $55.00 – 65.00.

Spine: Concentric Rings rooster pitcher, pg. 39, $35.00 – 40.00.

Back cover: Moroccan Alpine punch bowl set, pg. 185, $60.00 – 65.00.

Cover design • Beth Summers   Book design • Erica Weise

Cover Photography • Charles R. Lynch

COLLECTOR BOOKS

P.O. Box 3009
Paducah, Kentucky 42002-3009

www.collectorbooks.com

Gene and Cathy Florence

P.O. Box 22186
Lexington, KY 40522

P.O. Box 64
Astatula, FL 34705

Copyright © 2005 Gene and Cathy Florence

The current values in this book should be used only as a guide. They are not intended to set prices, which vary from one section of the country to another. Auction prices as well as dealer prices vary greatly and are affected by condition as well as demand. Neither the author nor the publisher assumes responsibility for any losses that might be incurred as a result of consulting this guide.

Searching For A Publisher?

We are always looking for people knowledgeable within their fields. If you feel that there is a real need for a book on your collectible subject and have a large comprehensive collection, contact Collector Books.

CONTENTS

ACKNOWLEDGMENTS

I want to particularly thank a forgotten named someone who approached me at a show wanting to know if I'd be interested in purchasing some Hazel-Atlas catalogs he'd found and "thought I might be the one to do something with them!" I wish to thank some fellow dealers who went out of their way to help discover and procure information and goods to be photographed or who secured photographs and mailed them to the studio. These include Dan and Geri Tucker; Charles and Sibyl Gaines; Glen and Carolyn Robinson; Dick and Pat Spencer; Jackie Morgan; Miles Bausch and Doug Lucas, owners of Miles-Douglas Galleries; Mary Frank Gaston; Dave and Kay Tucker; Robert and Marian Golden; Ben Harris; Dr. Francee S. Boches; and Ron and Barbara Marks.

I am indebted to all personally, and we, as collectors, are indebted to their efforts collectively. We hope we have contributed to the body of knowledge regarding this immense factory production over the years. We know there is much more to be learned, and look forward to discovering it either through our own continued efforts or someone else's.

PREFACE

When this book was first conceived, we thought we would have access to a 30-year collection of Hazel-Atlas wares and to neat things we had sold in the past to another long time collector. We thought we would have several more Hazel-Atlas catalogs than we wound up with and have the book finished long before now! As is the case in life, for myriad reasons, none of that worked out! People died, moved, couldn't find what they knew they had somewhere; so, we spent a couple of years doing this "the hard way," marching through malls, antique shops, junk stores, dawn flea markets, and friends' and relatives' cabinets, turning over glass to see if it was marked, pouring over the few catalogs and separate pages of information we'd unearthed, reading paragraphs and articles (of which there are apparently very few), trying to gather information and examples of glass products manufactured by Hazel-Atlas Glass Company. We, of course, were interested in their kitchen and tableware products initially; but it soon became VERY apparent that that would not suffice to tell the tale of this giant of glassware manufacturers whose products intertwined with everyday lives for over 70 years! They may have started out very humbly, making a lowly opal liner for a zinc lid, but by the 1930s, most households in America had their wares lining their medicine cabinets, their tables, their kitchen cabinets, their car

GEORGE WASHINGTON COMMEMORATIVE TUMBLER

1932 Sesquicentennial Anniversary Tumbler of George Washington's birth (1732), 4⅜"h x 3⅛"w at top; 2½" foot, topaz and green; relatively hard to find. **Green, $25.00 – 30.00.**

batteries and headlights, their radio tubes, their shoe polish cabinets, their desk drawers, and their pantry shelves. Indeed, many of the foods they ate arrived via Hazel-Atlas product packaging. The foods they diligently canned every summer were often "put up" in Hazel-Atlas fruit or canning jars. Hazel-Atlas company products were part and parcel of their everyday lives, though this was not at all noticed! You took all the medicine and tossed out the bottle the pharmacist bought from Hazel-Atlas. You rubbed on the Mentholatum or Vick's and did the same thing when that emptied, and so with ink, glue, shoe polish, cosmetic, cold cream, talcum powder, pickle, chili sauce, olive, cherry, mayonnaise, peanut butter, chipped beef, fish, or baby food jars. However, when the jelly tumblers, mustard, or shaving cups were emptied of their contents, they probably were saved and used again and again. They were "free" products in a time when frugality was both virtuous and necessary! Thus, today, many of these "useful" products' containers remain. Some that had survived their original use were swallowed up in WWII sweeps made to gather materials, cloth, tin, and glass for re-use in the war effort. For example, we looked long and hard at shelves of dug up bottles and found only one late example of a shoe polish container. Fortuitous for this book all these years later was a purchase I made 25 or more years ago of a huge stack of glass-related scrapbook type keepings of a former glassware salesman. Cathy recalled

there having been a typed notebook full of pages with an outside label saying "Hazel-Atlas." I'd completely forgotten about having it; indeed, I had read a few of what I then found to be tedious pages of ancient details when I first bought it and tossed it aside as having nothing relevant to offer my work then. Cathy unearthed it and spent days wading through the details, some quite technical, that the former employee had taken the time to write down about

his factory workings from its inception. As best she could, she pieced together a timeline summary of events from his writings gleaned from varying views of like details which may yield some of the more interesting historical data in the book. I also was able to borrow past finds from some of my own books to include herein. I did not bother to include them all in the bibliography, however — only the most recent ones.

HISTORY

In a history of Hazel-Atlas compiled by J. Alego, a former employee, the following data was presented, which we have attempted to condense into a timeline for quick reference. Unfortunately, the data only ran into the 1930s and was mostly concerned with their fruit jars and "packers container" business which was their major raison d'être. (For brevity, not all information is presented in complete sentences).

1885 (Sept. 3) – What was to become Hazel Glass Company was formed by C.N. Brady, president of Riverside Glass Co., and Chas. H. Tallman, secretary/treasurer of Bellaire Stamping Co. in Wellsburg, West Virginia. They each contributed $600.00 to obtain 2-day tanks to locate in a shed across the street from Riverside Glass Co. for the express purpose of making 1¼ oz. opal glass liners for Mason zinc caps which Bellaire Stamping Company made. It was too small of an account that Riverside supposedly found tedious and beneath their dignity as a tableware producing company to make a bottleware product of such insignificance. They purchased their first batches to make these tiny products from Riverside, wheeling it across the street to the tanks in wheelbarrows.

1886 (March) – Brady's sister-in-law named the stack "Hazel," following a tradition in the steel industry at the time to name their blast furnaces. She supposedly just picked the name at random.

1886 – Moved to Washington, Pennsylvania. Natural gas supplies playing out in Wellsburg and business expanding. The Washington city fathers donated land for a bigger plant; now have 4-day tanks and are pressing opal jars for ointments and patch boxes for salves. It is believed that this is first time such opal containers were made available to market. First glass produced there on Jan. 10, 1887. Made first hollow ware fruit jars, oil cans, molasses cans, lamp bases, and chimneys in this plant. Oil cans were gallon sized and used in most homes, which did not yet have newfangled electricity. Big business! Fruit jars were now made with a pressed neck into which a jar was blown and hacked off from a punty stick. This is opposite the previous manner of blowing the jar first and then affixing a neck ring. Due to grinding off tops, nothing could seal hermetically. No standardized jar caps. Caps made to fit each jar.

1888 (June 12) – First container made at new Hazel Plant No. 1, which boasted a 12-pot furnace. Two opal tanks added 1889 when old factory abandoned. An eight-pot furnace added 1892.

1892 (Sept. 1) – Assets for Hazel listed at $88,635.58 by Mr. Brady. With flint (clear) glass which took a longer cooking time, at optimum could gross 20 quart jars of production per day, a maximum of 660 per furnace over the 5½ day work week. (Green glass production of other companies could possibly double this figure as it took half the time to prepare green glass). In making flint only half the pots could be worked at one time and they could only be worked during the day. Glass was shipped in wooden containers packed with hay, straw, sawdust, or wood chips via railroad and wagon.

1892 – Mr. Brady commissioned the making of a kind of automated jar-making machine he'd had an idea for but needed help implementing.

1893 – Cleveland Panic. Business went down fast. Is said Mr. Brady pledged his life insurance to keep his workers paid. Began making bottles for catsup, maple syrup, and chili sauce, casting about for new business.

1894 – The "Blue" machine (made by Charles Blue, of Wheeling Mold and Foundry) was finally patented Dec. 25, 1894, to make a completed jar on each revolving of a wheel from 5 molds on a rotating table — the "merry-go-round" rotary press. Speeded up production considerably. Reduced number of workers needed. Sales from wide-mouthed fruit jars, opal Mason liners, and pressed containers for medicines, salves, and ointments equaled $250,000!

1894 – The continuous lehr is taking over for the annealing ovens in use in the industry. Hazel had always used lehrs from the beginning; but these were state of the art now, reducing the time required to anneal to 4 – 5 hours, rather than the old Monday through Thursday process of the ovens. Same day packaging of wares was now possible.

1894 – Hazel makes first Phoenix (cap) finish jar for use with jams and jellies, their #80 jar being the most popular. Invented in France in 1892 and shown at 1893 World's Fair by Alfred Weissanthanner, the cap was one use and machine applied and was made in standard sizes of 48, 53, 58, and 63 m/m. Resulted in standardization of jar neck sizes in industry. No more making caps to fit jars of whatever size; now jar necks fit caps. Among first packers to use the Phoenix finish jar for Hazel were Chesebrough Mfg. Co, Carter's Ink, Reid Murdock and Co., and Sprague Warner Co.

1895 – Hazel first used the wondrous, new, continuous tank to feed glass to molds. Now melting and working glass are one operation. Batch fed in one end and worked out the other. Permitted day and night operation. No more running out of batch mid-day when working larger objects, bringing operations to a halt until the next batch of glass had cooked out in the pots and was ready to be worked.

1896 (July 20) – Mr. Brady, along with R.J. and George Beatty and J.W. Paxton form Atlas Glass Company for the express purpose of taking over the making of fruit jars and leaving Hazel "everything else," i.e., jars for Vaseline, inks, shoe polishes, jams, pickles, etc. Made the cheaper green glass jars there because that's what the competition was using. Also had blowers there making bottles for mineral water because the Blue machine wasn't able to make smaller necked bottles.

1896 –1900 – All sorts of litigation over infringement use of Blue machine technology. Courts deemed patent from prior Danish design of 1889 had run its course by 1900 and machine was fair game from then on.

1899 – Wheeling Metal Company formed in order to make zinc caps for both Hazel and Atlas. Later they made screw caps from tin, aluminum, and brass.

1900 – On a rotary machine known as the Cleveland Press, the Republic Glass Company, founded by brother of C.N. Brady (which later became the Clarksburg Plant for Hazel), made tumblers with an automated plunger with a glazed edge which were so superior to the old, rough, ground, sharp-edged tumblers, that the railroad placed a premium on the shipment of these "jelly (packers) jars," labeling them as tableware and charging a higher fee.

1901 – Hazel picked up lucrative amber snuff bottle business from U.S. Tobacco. Sometime prior to this had gotten the Mentholatum jar making business.

1902 – All above-mentioned plants associated with Hazel became Hazel-Atlas.

1903 – Giles vacuum cap increased container sales for chipped beef, shredded codfish, sliced bacon, and peanut butter.

1904 – Built Hazel-Atlas #3 to make small-necked olive and cherry jars.

1904 – Fully automated Owens Machine appeared and dominated the business because it sucked glass into the mold by vacuum, the machine rotated continuously rather than intermittently, glass flowed directly from the tank into a revolving pot from which it was sucked into the mold, and it could make both jars and bottles at a precise sameness of weight and configuration. Did away with seven jobs in the making of bottles and three in the making of jars, thereby cutting production costs. Further, they doled out licenses, which dictated which company could make what product on their machine. Thatcher could make milk bottles; Illinois and Chas. Bolt glass and liquor bottles; Hazel could make wide mouthed bottles for the packing trade only, excluding them from fruit jars which Greenfield (later Ball) was allowed to make. They were allowed to continue their previous wide-mouthed Vaseline and Vick's jars, their snuff bottles and wide mouthed cosmetic jars and other areas established prior to their entering into contract for the Owens machine. Cost them the up and coming Hellman's Mayonnaise business. Hazel installed Owen's Machines in 1909. Could eventually make four bottles in one mold with multiple cavities. The bulk of their packers jars from ½ pint up were made on Owens Machines until they became obsolete by 1931.

1904 – Tumbler-shaped jars for packing everything from meats to jellies made at Clarksburg plant and for 25 – 30 years. Also was the tableware plant, shipping everything F.O.B. that plant. In one mention, Mr. Algeo says two-mold pressed nappies (Old English term for round vessel), pitchers, goblets, and tumblers were coming from the Clarksburg plant as early as 1904. In another, he says nappies and mixing bowls were produced there around 1921.

1905 – The Hermetic Closure Company was formed of which Hazel-Atlas had ⅓ interest. Hazel made all glass containers using this closure except for fruit jars.

1906 – Jars advertised for packer's trade as "conforming to the Pure Foods Act of 1906." This came from outcry over soldiers dying from canned poisoned meats during the Spanish–American War. After that 1895 disaster, any container product was viewed badly by public and it affected sales adversely. Federal law came into being to regulate the industry much to chagrin of shysters packing inferior (and/or "spoiled") products.

1907 – Mrs. Schlorer of Philadelphia decided to package her delicatessen mayonnaise in Hazel-Atlas packing jars and business took off until the 1920s when it was being overtaken by Hellman's.

1909 – First use of paper cases for packaging fruit jars by Hazel-Atlas, a practice begun by Ball in 1907. Soon after, sold cases of 12 jars which included the cap and rubber gasket seal.

1911 – Hermetic bought Phoenix Cap and became Phoenix Hermetic Company. (You've heard of something being "hermetically sealed?")

1914 – Panama Canal opened, resulting in cheaper rates for products shipped to West Coast.

1915 – Frenchman Duval, chemist, hired as laborer on wheelbarrow duty at Hazel-Atlas Clarksburg plant noticed the muddy green resulting from manganese shortage (war) used to "clear" it and pestered the foreman to let him make it a good clear color. Finally, he was allowed to try and added a "secret" ingredient and got clear glass —- which held clear rather than turning purple or pink in two days as did the manganese guesswork route. They finally discovered it was selenium he was adding.

1915 – 1916 – Significant amber bottle order from England for Bovril beef extract and snuff.

1916 – Armed forces ordered masses of 20 oz. syrup bottles, resulting in big sales.

1916 – Grafton plant opened with one tank; a second was added by 1917.

1917 - Backed into blue Vick's Vaporub jar business because smaller Maryland factory subsidiary making them couldn't keep up with the orders because of the flu epidemic sweeping the country.

1917 – 1918 – Employed a crew specifically to locate the shipped soda and ash products needed to produce the glass lost by a near breakdown of the railroad business due to the war.

1918 – Hazel-Atlas bought its own timber to use for boxing; sold it in 1924 with the increasing use of paper for shipping.

1919 – Total volume of glass containers was 22,227,000.

1919 – Hazelcap, shallow, vacuum seal cap with easy twist-off feature, and paper cases for shipping resulted in freight cost saving.

1920 – Owned 22 tanks, some west of Mississippi, (Oklahoma Glass and Bottle). On Jan. 1, Prohibition nearly decimated the bottle industry; Oct. 20 financial market crash resulted in a 47% decline in business volume.

1920 – Mrs. Fanning decided to can (not soak in brine for weeks) nubbins and culls of cucumbers with a spice recipe given her by her mother. She cooked and preserved them in Mason jars with zinc lids and sold them locally. It took off, and everybody loved them. Mr. Fanning didn't care for the look of that jar and picked a Hazel-Atlas one. After trial and error with some spoilage, they sold these bread and butter pickles far and wide using four railroad carloads of jars. Pickles called "bread and butter" because Mrs. Fanning told someone that those pickles tasted good "with bread and butter."

1920 – Mr. Clapp of Rochester, New York, who owned a restaurant, noticed the inordinate amount of time his wife spent fixing food for their four youngsters. He got the idea of running the stuff through his puree machine, which delighted the Mrs., and all her friends whom she told. He decided to prepare this commercially. He chose the Hazel-Atlas pint jar and distributed his baby food through dairies. He started a factory in 1926 and chose the Hazel-Atlas 5-ounce tumbler. In 1931, he sold the business to Johnson and Johnson who went to cans. Beech-nut stayed with glass when they got into the business and ultimately chose a jar from Hazel-Atlas, which became a standard in the industry.

1921 – A few nappies and mixing bowls were being produced at the Clarksburg plant.

1922 – Two tanks were added to make more opal cosmetic type jars, but they were kept in the medicine line of the catalog until 1928 when they finally headed them under "cosmetics" containers. Cosmetic business was becoming a force in the economic picture.

1925 – 23,410,000 gross containers sold. Officially recovered from economic downturn.

1927 – Butler Bros. Catalog advertised opal kitchenware line in their catalog listings.

1928 – Advertised as the "World's Largest Tumbler Factory." (I believe Economy was known to claim this title as well).

1929 – Spring, a boom year! New plant opened in San Francisco. Due to competition, had had to absorb freight costs to West Coast the last several years. Now, could produce there and compete in that zone. Except for tableware business, could charge freight on zone basis. Tablewares were still F.O.B. factory at Clarksburg, something of a sore point as was contrary to shipping standards of the other wares —- a practice "inherited" from the early 1900s.

1929 – Added lines of colored green tableware to its catalog.

1929 (Oct.) – Financial crash ushering in the Great Depression. Unlike the 20s crash, didn't pull out of it in two or three years. Was six or seven before things were going well again. Took in less in 1930 than had in 1920, $19,805,000.00. Estimated prices declined over 40%.

1930s – Plants on West Coast are mostly self-contained, with good sources of oil, natural gas, sand, and ash, obviating the need to bring raw materials from Belgium, a process that had proved difficult during WWI.

1933 – Had added Opal, Topaz and, by 1935, Rose (pink) and black tableware lines to customer offerings.

Mid-1930s – Introduction of the "White" screw cap, the "cat's meow" of tops, still being used when plant was sold in 1956. Would seal and screw off and on with ease.

1936 – Shirley Temple items made for General Mills food company as premiums in what was advertised by them as "lovely Sapphire Blue" glass.

1936 – Ad in Louisville Tin and Stove Company catalog shows the Diamond Optic, Moderntone, and Horseshoe tumblers offered to store owners in crystal, green, and rose for $3.60 for 4 dozen. The Horseshoe was a plain packing jar tumbler shown in an early 1900s ad. Then you could buy a dozen for less than 20 cents.

1937 – Ushered in a cobalt or "Ritz" blue tableware line. Forty-four pieces of either Royal Lace or Moderntone could be bought in 1938 for $2.99 according to advertisements in a Missouri newspaper of the time. Also some pieces of amethyst or burgundy appeared. Scuttlebutt has it they were trying to make red, but couldn't hold the color and wound up with this now considered rare color. Whether that is truth or legend we don't know. Early amethyst pieces are few and far between.

1930s, 1940s, and 1950s – Continuation of made-to-order product jars, tumblers, and tablewares for specific companies and markets, i.e. Crisco, Maxwell House, Burma – Shave, and Bisquick; orders for "premium product" containers grew during Depression Era as firms fought for the few dollars available; large percentage of business still containers, but by 1950s, plastic industry making inroads. Plants aging, costs of basic materials rising; unions; shipping, storage. In short, costs going up and usage of glass materials slipping in favor of cheaper plastic containers.

1956 – Sold to Continental Can Company; sale held up seven years until the courts decided it wasn't a monopoly in 1963. During this interim, products were continued to be sold as Hazel-Atlas products, albeit through catalogs marked as distributed by Continental Can; and beyond that time, at least into the 1970s, they were sold as Hazelware products. We have a florist catalog dated 1970 showing both opal and avocado green floral wares offered for sale that year — one of which was the 7" crimped top, ribbed middle tumbler vase (Catalog #W-388), which we know was an early 1930s green glass offering.

HOW TO USE PHOTO LEGENDS

To make this book easier to use and to provide more information, you will find photo legends in the pattern section, starting on page 143. Each piece is identified through the use of photo legends on large group shots. Each piece is numbered in the photo legends with corresponding numbers alongside the listings. You can tell exactly what piece is in the photo, and then refer to the listing to find size, color, price, and other information.

	Bowl, 4¾", berry	$3.50
⑤	Creamer	$4.50
②	Cup	$3.50
	Plate, 6", sherbet	$1.50
①	Plate, 8", luncheon	$2.50
	Plate, 9", dinner	$3.50
	Platter, 11"	$7.50
	Salt and pepper, pr.	$15.00
④	Saucer	$1.00
⑰	Sherbet	$5.50
⑥	Sugar, open	$4.50
⑫	Tumbler	$12.00

Glassware – "Ash Trays"

by **HAZEL-ATLAS**

1273–4½'' Star Ash
Tray
Pkd. 6 doz. ctn. Wt. 28 lbs.
Height 1⁵⁄₁₆''

9785–4½'' Square Ash
Tray
Pkd. 4 doz. ctn. Wt. 19 lbs.
Height 1¹⁄₁₆''

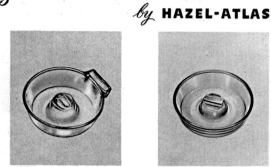

9772–4¾'' No-Mess-Er
Ash Tray
Pkd. 4 doz. ctn. Wt. 30 lbs.
Height 1⁹⁄₃₂''

9830–4½'' No-Mess-Er
Ash Tray
Pkd. 4 doz. ctn. Wt. 22 lbs.
Height 1³⁄₃₂''

596–3½'' Square
Ash Tray
Pkd. 4 doz. ctn. Wt. 14 lbs.
Height 1³⁄₁₆''

597–4⅝'' Square
Ash Tray
Pkd. 4 doz. ctn. Wt. 27 lbs.
Height 1¼''

598–5⅜'' Square
Ash Tray
Pkd. 2 doz. ctn. Wt. 30 lbs.
Height 1⁹⁄₁₆''

623–4'' Square
Ash Tray–Lightweight
Pkd. 4 doz. ctn. Wt. 19 lbs.
Height ⅞''

551–4'' Heavy Square
Ash Tray
Pkd. 4 doz. ctn. Wt. 52 lbs.
Height 1⁹⁄₃₂''

556–3¾'' Heavy Square
Ash Tray
Pkd. 4 doz. ctn. Wt. 43 lbs.
Height 1¼''

557–3¾'' Heavy Square
Ash Tray
Pkd. 4 doz. ctn. Wt. 50 lbs.
Height 1½''

386–4½'' ''Sentinel''
Ash Tray
Pkd. 2 doz. ctn. Wt. 15 lbs.
Height 1⁵⁄₁₆''

957–5'' x 2½'' x 1'' Oblong
Ash Tray
Pkd. 4 doz. ctn. Wt. 24 lbs.
Height 1³⁄₁₆''

961–6'' x 4'' x 1½'' Oblong
Ash Tray
Pkd. 4 doz. ctn. Wt. 46 lbs.
Height 1½''

990–7'' x 5'' x 1¾'' Oblong
Ash Tray
Pkd. 2 doz. ctn. Wt. 40 lbs.
Height 1¹¹⁄₁₆''

491–3½'' x 5'' Modern
Swedish Ash Tray
Pkd. 2 doz. ctn. Wt. 16 lbs.
Height 1³⁄₁₆''

FROM *GLASSWARE BY HAZEL-ATLAS CATALOG, 1957,* **PAGE 17.**

AMETHYST

BLOSSOM – Cat. #289, sq., 3½", with or without label, **$8.00 – 10.00.**

COLONY SQUARE – 8" plate tray, **$12.00 – 14.00.**

DAISY – Nesting Set,   Cat. #492, 3¼", **$4.00 – 5.00.**
                     Cat. #493, $4^{11}\!/_{32}$", **$5.00 – 6.00.**
                     Cat. #494, 5½", **$6.00 – 8.00.**

TRIANGLE – Cigar Tray, 6⅞", **$9.00 – 10.00.**

TRIANGLE – Individual rounded tip, **$5.00.**

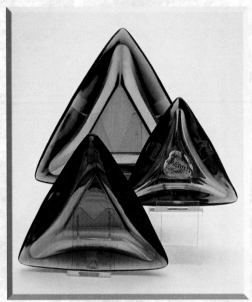

TRIANGLE – Nesting set,   3⅞", **$5.00 – 6.00.**
                       4⅞", **$7.00 – 8.00.**
                       6", **$9.00 – 10.00.**

BLUE

CAPRI BLOSSOM
Cat. #289, sq., 3½", **$8.00 – 10.00.**

CAPRI TRIANGLE
Cigar, large, 6⅞", **$9.00 – 10.00.**

TRIANGLE
6", from nesting set, **$8.00 – 9.00.**

COASTER – 3¼", **$7.00 – 8.00.**

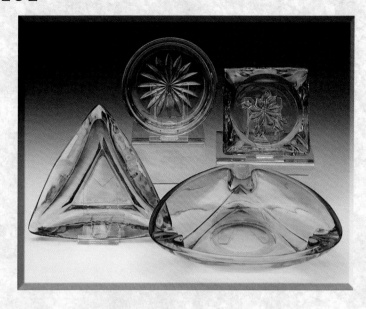

SHELL
Platonite blue or pink, **$6.00 – 7.00 each.**

"SHIPS"
Round or square with silver trim, **$25.00 – 30.00 each.**

"NO-MESS-ER"
Cat. #9772, with handle, 1⁹⁄₃₂"h x 4¾"w.
$25.00 – 30.00.

Not shown:
Crystal, **$10.00 – 12.00.**
Green, **$15.00 – 18.00.**

"STAR IN STAR"
Cat. #549, 5" point to point.
$10.00 – 12.00.

Not shown:
Crystal, **$6.00 – 8.00.**

CRYSTAL

BUCKET – No mark, 2⅜"h, **$2.00 – 3.00.**

BARREL
Jigger/toothpick/cigarette holder/ashtray,
Cat. #169, 2⅜", 1¾ oz., **$4.00 – 5.00.**

Also available in green and gold. Shown in Hazel-Atlas catalog, pg. 47.

"NO-MESS-ER"
Without handle, Cat. #9830.
1 9/32" h x 4¾" w, plain, **$8.00 – 9.00.**
With advertising, **$30.00 – 35.00.**

SQUARE COASTER/ASHTRAY
Cat. #815, 3⅜", **$6.00 – 8.00.**

FLUTED ROUND – Nesting set
Cat. #967, 3⅛"w x 3 1/32"h , **$3.00 – 4.00.**
Cat. #968, 4¼"w x 1⅛"h, **$4.00 – 5.00.**
Cat. #969, 5½"w x 1⅛"h, **$5.00 – 6.00.**

GREEN

TRIANGLE STARS
Cat. #757½ with match holder, 4" embossed.
Green, **$10.00 – 12.00.**

Not shown:
Crystal, **$6.00 – 7.00.**

RAYED CENTER
Cat. #758, 5¾".
Green, **$12.00 – 15.00.**

TRIANGLE STARS
Cat. #757, 4" embossed.
Crystal, **$4.00 – 5.00.**

Not shown:
Green, **$8.00 – 10.00.**

SEE ASHTRAYS IN **NEW CENTURY** PATTERN, PAGES 188 AND 189.

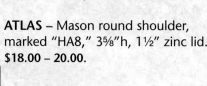

MINIATURE ATLAS HA BANK – Mason square shoulder, marked "HA8," 3⁹⁄₁₆"h, Seal-All arc lid, **$18.00 – 20.00.**

ATLAS – Mason round shoulder, marked "HA8," 3⅝"h, 1½" zinc lid. **$18.00 – 20.00.**

Both shown with regular sized jar

ATLAS
Large 2 quart mason canning jar, #5062 C, **$10.00 – 15.00.**

BOSCO BEAR – Marked "2" and "HA8" on bottom with Bosco name forming cross, 7½"h, **$20.00 – 25.00.**

BOSCO CLOWN
Marked "HA," 7½"h, **$20.00 – 25.00.**

LUCKY JOE – Sometimes described as "Donald Duck," marked "HA8," held 8½ oz. of prepared mustard from the Nash-Underwood Co. Chicago, 4½"h, **$25.00 – 30.00.**

FRUITETTE SODA CLOWN – marked "HA" (Other versions of this soda bank, i.e. elephant, fox, bear; also made by other manufacturers. Arkansas company made this soda), **$15.00 – 20.00.** With syrup, **$45.00.**

 *Bar Ware* by **HAZEL-ATLAS**

56—⅝ oz. Small Tumbler
Whisky
Pkd. 6 doz. ctn. Wt. 24 lbs.
Height 2²³⁄₃₂" Top 1¾" Base 1⁵⁄₁₆"

516—¾ oz. Small Tumbler
Whisky
Pkd. 6 doz. ctn. Wt. 22 lbs.
Height 2⅞" Top 1¾" Base 1⁵⁄₁₆"

9630—⅞ oz. Small Tumbler
Whisky
Pkd. 6 doz. ctn. Wt. 21 lbs.
Height 2⅞" Top 1¾" Base 1⁵⁄₁₆"

9547—1 oz. Small Tumbler
Whisky
Pkd. 6 doz. ctn. Wt. 19 lbs.
Height 2⅞" Top 1¾" Base 1⁵⁄₁₆"

522—1 oz. Small Tumbler
Whisky
Pkd. 6 doz. ctn. Wt. 37 lbs.
Height 3³⁄₁₆" Top 2" Base 1⁷⁄₁₆"

521—1¼ oz. Small Tumbler
Whisky
Pkd. 6 doz. ctn. Wt. 34 lbs.
Height 3³⁄₁₆" Top 2" Base 1⁷⁄₁₆"

9752—1½ oz. Small Tumbler
Whisky
Pkd. 6 doz. ctn. Wt. 32 lbs.
Height 3³⁄₁₆" Top 2" Base 1¹⁵⁄₃₂"

9588—2 oz. Small Tumbler
Whisky
Pkd. 6 doz. ctn. Wt. 26 lbs.
Height 3³⁄₁₆" Top 2" Base 1⅜"

519—⅝ oz. Small Tumbler
Whisky
Pkd. 6 doz. ctn. Wt. 24 lbs.
Height 2²¹⁄₆₄" Top 1¹⁵⁄₁₆" Base 1¼"

520—¾ oz. Small Tumbler
Whisky
Pkd. 6 doz. ctn. Wt. 23 lbs.
Height 2¹¹⁄₃₂" Top 1³¹⁄₃₂" Base 1¹¹⁄₃₂"

208—⅞ oz. Small Tumbler
Whisky
Pkd. 6 doz. ctn. Wt. 23 lbs.
Height 2¹⁷⁄₆₄" Top 2⅛" Base 1³⁄₁₆"

489—1 oz. Small Tumbler
Whisky
Pkd. 6 doz. ctn. Wt. 21 lbs.
Height 2¹¹⁄₃₂" Top 1¹⁵⁄₁₆" Base 1¹¹⁄₃₂"

616—1 oz. Small Tumbler
Whisky
Pkd. 6 doz. ctn. Wt. 22 lbs.
Height 2¼" Top 2⁵⁄₃₂" Base 1⁵⁄₁₆"

458—1⅜ oz. Small Tumbler
Whisky
Pkd. 6 doz. ctn. Wt. 15 lbs.
Height 2¼" Top 1⅞" Base 1¹¹⁄₃₂"

457 (†457½)—1 oz. Small Tumbler
Whisky
Pkd. 6 doz. ctn. Wt. 14 lbs.
Height 2¼" Top 1⅞" Base 1⅜"

1589—1½ oz. Small Tumbler
Whisky
Pkd. 6 doz. ctn. Wt. 7 lbs.
Height 2¼" Top 1¹¹⁄₁₆" Base 1⁷⁄₃₂"

†Item numbers within ( ) in light face type are the former numbers

FROM *GLASSWARE BY HAZEL-ATLAS* CATALOG, 1957, PAGE 8.

RITZ BLUE – C.1938

THESE SPORTS-RELATED ITEMS WERE MARKETED UNDER
THE MASCULINE SOUNDING **"SPORTSMAN SERIES."**

"ANGEL FISH"
Ice bowl, **$50.00 – 60.00.**
Cocktail shaker, **$45.00 – 55.00.**
Fruit juice, 5 oz., **$10.00 – 12.00.**
Highball tumbler, 10 oz., **$12.00 – 15.00.**

"FLAGS" ("Ships' Flags")
Cocktail shaker, 10", **$40.00 – 50.00.**
Fruit juice, 5 oz., **$8.00 – 12.00.**
Highball tumbler, (shown) 10 oz., **$10.00 – 15.00.**
(Also found in crystal with red flags).

"FANCY SHIPS" – With white cloud rings, cocktail shaker, **$70.00 – 80.00;**
old-fashioned whiskey, **$12.00 – 15.00;** ice tub, 44 oz., **$40.00 – 50.00;** fruit
juice (not shown), 5 oz., **$10.00 – 12.00.**

"LEASHED AFGHAN HOUND & SCOTTIE"
Ice tub, 44 oz., **$60.00 – 70.00.**
with stand and tongs, **$75.00 – 85.00.**
Highball tumbler, 10 oz., **$18.00 – 22.00.**

"HUNT SCENE" ("Tally Ho")
Old-fashioned whiskey, **$12.00 – 15.00.**
Cocktail shaker, **$50.00 – 60.00.**

Not shown:
Juice, 5 oz., **$14.00 – 16.00.**

RITZ BLUE – C.1938

"RINGS O RINGS"
Decanter with sequentially numbered whiskey tumblers. Unmarked, traditionally ascribed to Hazel-Atlas and reputed to have once held bath salts.
Decanter, **$30.00 – 35.00.**
Whiskey, **$6.00 – 8.00.**

"SAILOR" ("Dancing Sailor")
   Ice tub, **$60.00 – 75.00.**
   Highball tumbler, **$22.00 – 25.00.**

Not shown:
   Cocktail shaker, **$150.00 – 175.00.**
Also available with rope design – rarely seen.

"SHIPS" – White Ship, Dec. #420,
   Tea, 12 oz., **$13.00 – 15.00.**
   Highball or tall table tumbler, 10 oz., **$14.00 – 16.00.**
   Table, 9 oz., **$10.00 – 12.00.**
   Fruit juice, 5 oz., **$13.00 – 15.00.**
   Roly poly, 6 oz. punch or whiskey, **$10.00 – 12.00.**
   Old-fashioned whiskey, 8 oz., 3⅜", **$18.00 – 20.00.**
   Whiskey, heavy bottom/indented side, 4 oz., 3¼", **$22.00 – 28.00.**
   Shot tumbler, 2 oz., 2¼", **$200.00 – 250.00.**

Not shown:
   Cocktail mixer pail (with rim), Cat. #9651, **$25.00 – 30.00.**
   Cocktail mixer spoon/muddler, **$5.00 – 8.00.**
      Ice tub, 4¼"h x 5½"w, 44 oz., **$45.00 – 55.00.**
         with metal tongs, **$75.00.**
      Tea, 15 oz., **$35.00 – 40.00.**

Cocktail shaker, 10", **$50.00 – 60.00.**

RITZ BLUE – C.1938

"WINDMILL" – Cat. #9651
    Highball tumbler, 10 oz., **$14.00 – 16.00.**
    Whiskey, heavy bottom/indent side, **$18.00 – 20.00.**
    Cocktail shaker, 10", **$40.00 – 50.00.**
    Old-fashioned whiskey, 8 oz., 3⅜", **$16.00 – 18.00.**
    Ice pail with rim, **$30.00 – 35.00.**
    Roly Poly whiskey, **$12.00 – 15.00.**

Not shown:
    Cocktail mixer spoon/muddler, **$5.00 – 8.00.**
    Fruit juice, 5 oz., **$10.00 – 12.00.**

THIS DESIGN IS EASIER TO
FIND THAN OTHERS SHOWN.

NOTE: COCKTAIL SHAKERS SOMETIMES
CAME WITH RED BAKELITE TYPE
STOPPERS AND WERE PRESENTED ON
TRAYS WITH MATCHING RED HANDLES.
THE BAKELITE STOPPER IS OFTEN
MISSING WHERE IT HARDENED AND
BROKE OVER THE YEARS.

"WHITE RINGS"
    Highball tumbler, 10 oz., **$10.00 – 12.00.**
    Old-fashioned whiskey, 8 oz., 3⅜", **$12.00 – 14.00.**
    Bowl, ice, cereal type, **$22.00 – 25.00.**
    Whiskey, heavy bottom/indented side, 4 oz., 3¼", **$14.00 – 18.00.**
    Fruit juice, 5 oz., **$8.00 – 10.00.**

ICE BOWLS AND TUBS

"BLOCKS DESIGN"
Cat. #647, 49 oz., 4¾"h x 5¾"w,
$18.00 – 20.00.

Not shown:
Highball tumbler, $6.00 – 8.00.
Cocktail shaker, $25.00 – 30.00.

"HATS DESIGN" – Ice tub, 44 oz.,
5½" diam., $20.00 – 25.00.

RIBBED ICE (MIXING) BOWLS
Various types, with silver
holders and tongs.
6⅝", $35.00 – 40.00.
7⅝", $35.00 – 40.00.
8⅝", $45.00 – 50.00.
9⅝", $50.00 – 55.00.
10⅝", $85.00 – 95.00.
11⅝", $110.00 – 125.00.
(With holder and tongs, add $10.00 – 15.00 to value.)

ICE TUBS WITH MATCHING TUMBLERS

"HUNT SCENE JUMP"
Whiskey tumbler, 3⅛", HA mark, $6.00 – 8.00.
Ice tub, 44 oz., 4¼"h x 5½" diam, $40.00 – 45.00.

Not shown:
Pitcher, 80 oz. Concentric Ring (neck & base), $60.00 – 65.00.
Highball tumbler, $8.00 – 10.00.

ICE TUBS WITH MATCHING TUMBLERS

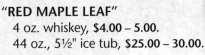

"KENTUCKY DERBY WINNERS"
1930s – 1940s, highball tumbler, **$10.00-12.00 each.**
Ice tub, Cat. #647, **$60.00 – 70.00.**

"RED MAPLE LEAF"
4 oz. whiskey, **$4.00 – 5.00.**
44 oz., 5½" ice tub, **$25.00 – 30.00.**

"POLAR BEAR" – With Frost decoration
Highball tumbler, **$8.00 – 10.00.**
Ice tub, 44 oz., 5½" diam., **$55.00 – 65.00.**

Not shown:
Cocktail shaker, **$75.00 – 100.00.**
Whiskey tumbler, marked, **$8.00 – 10.00.**

FROST DECORATIONS WITHOUT THE BEAR CAN BE FOUND ON REFRIGERATOR JARS.

"SCHOONERS"
Highball tumblers, 5", **$6.00 – 8.00 each.**
Ice tub, 44 oz., 4¾"h x 5¾"w, Cat. #647, **$20.00 –25.00.**
Linda of New York - Mar. 30; 1858.
John Bibby of Liverpool - Feb. 4, 1858, (Tub).
Emperor of New Orleans - 1845.

Also Available:
St. Lawrence of Glasgow - Feb. 23, 1858.
Kate Howe of Medford - 1847.

"GAY NINETIES"
Highball tumblers, 6", **$6.00 – 8.00** each.
Tray, metal, 13¼", **$20.00 – 25.00.**
Cocktail shaker, 10", **$25.00 – 30.00.**
Whiskey, marked, 3¹/₁₆"h, **$6.00 – 8.00** each.

"GEESE FLYING"
5" tumbler, **$5.00 – 6.00.**

"MOROCCAN AMETHYST" – Hazelware, c. 1960s, cocktail shaker, **$30.00 – 35.00**; whiskey, 2½", **$6.00 – 8.00**; set in box, **$85.00 – 95.00.**

"MUSICAL" – Clef, guitar, horns, drums.
Highball tumbler, 5¹/₁₆"h, **$8.00 – 10.00.**
Whiskey tumbler, 4 oz., 3⅛", **$6.00 – 8.00.**
Old-fashioned whiskey tumbler, 3¹/₁₆", **$6.00 – 8.00.**

Not shown:
Cocktail shaker, **$30.00 – 35.00.**

"TALLY HO"
Cocktail shaker, 10⅛", **$25.00 – 30.00.**
Highball tumbler, 6⅜", **$7.00 – 9.00.**

Not shown:
Tumbler, 5⅛", **$6.00 – 8.00.**
Whiskey, 3⅛", 4 oz., **$5.00 – 6.00.**

COCKTAIL SETS

"PHEASANTS"
Cocktail shaker,
   Sham (heavy) bottom, $30.00 – 35.00.
Highball tumbler,
   Sham (heavy) bottom, 5", $6.00 – 8.00.

"PHEASANTS"
Pheasant tumbler with hunter.
   5", flat bottom, $5.00 – 6.00.
34 oz. pitcher, $25.00 – 28.00.
Also available:
   Pheasant 5" tumbler with black
   and white bird dog, $8.00 – 10.00.

PITCHER POSSIBLY BARTLETT-COLLINS CO. HAZEL-ATLAS #391 VERSION SHAPED THUS USUALLY CAME WITH FINGERGRIP HANDLE AS SEEN ON MUGS, PAGE 31.

ONE TUMBLER HAZEL-ATLAS; ONE CONTINENTAL CAN WITH "1959 VETERAN'S BANQUET" IN GOLD LETTERING.

"PHEASANTS"
Cocktail shaker, flat bottom, $30.00 – 35.00.
Shot whiskey tumbler, 1½ oz., $3.00 – 5.00.
Pitcher with ice lip, 80 oz.,
   Concentric Rings, 9½", $40.00 – 45.00.
Ice tub, with hunter, 3¾"h x 5¾",
   Cat. #647, $20.00 – 25.00.

Not shown:
   Whiskey sham (heavy) bottom, 4 oz., 3⅛", $4.00 – 6.00.

"PINK ELEPHANT"
Ice tub, 44 oz., 5½" diam., $45.00 – 55.00.
Old-fashioned whiskey, $20.00 – 22.00.
Fruit juice, 5 oz., $14.00 – 16.00.
Cocktail shaker, $65.00 – 75.00.

Not shown:
   Mug,
      Concentric Rings, $30.00 – 35.00.
   Pilsner, 10 oz., $80.00 – 90.00.
   Shot, $12.00 – 15.00.
   Tea, $12.00 – 14.00.
   Water, $10.00 – 12.00.
   Whiskey, 4 oz., $18.00 – 20.00.

SHAKERS WITH PLASTIC LIDS

"MIXED DRINKS"
Instructions for eight drinks:
*Whiskey Sour, Martini, Manhattan,
Bacardi, Alexander, Daiquiri, Bronx,*
and *Side Car.*
6⅝"h x 3¾"w, marked, **$15.00 – 18.00.**

"FLORAL LEAVES"
6⅝"h x 3¾"w, **$10.00 – 12.00.**
"BACHELOR BUTTON"
Red, 6⅝"h x 3¾"w, **$10.00 – 12.00.**

OLD CARS

OLD CARS – Highball tumblers, 5⅛", **$4.00 – 6.00 each.**

OLD CARS

"OLD AUTOS" OR "OLD TIMERS"
 4 oz. shell bar tumblers,
 Ford Model T, **$5.00 – 6.00 each.**
 10 oz. tumblers, like Chevrolet,
  Frosted or clear, **$5.00 – 7.00 each.**

"OLD AUTOS" OR "OLD TIMERS"
 Gay Fad Studios Designs
  Whiskey tumblers, 4 oz., **$5.00 – 6.00 each.**

SERIES: 1904 Oldsmobile, 1900 Packard, 1903 Rambler, 1914 Dodge, 1910 Ford, 1911 Buick, 1912 Chevrolet, and 1903 Cadillac.

"OLD AUTOS" OR "OLD TIMERS"
 Cocktail shaker, 6⅝"h x 3¾"w, with plastic top, **$15.00 – 18.00.**
 Whiskey, marked Hazel-Atlas, 3⅜", curved bottom, **$4.00 – 6.00.**
 Whiskey, marked Hazel-Atlas, 3¼", sham bottom, **$4.00 – 6.00.**

Not shown:
 Highball tumbler, 5⅛", **$4.00 – 6.00.**
 Mixer with lip, 16 oz., **$18.00 – 20.00.**
 Cocktail with chrome top, 32 oz., **$25.00 – 30.00.**
 Decanter, **$20.00 – 22.00.**

SERIES: Ford, Chevrolet, Studebaker, Cadillac, Buick, Packard, Oldsmobile, Hudson.

WHISKEY TUMBLERS

"#521"
Small shot, whiskey, 1¼ oz.
$3.00 – 4.00.
Shown on catalog page 14.

"CAPRI OLD-FASHIONED"
  $6.00 – 8.00.

WHISKEY TUMBLERS

"A VOTRE SANTE; SALUD; SKOL; TO YOUR HEALTH"
    "Hand" ice tub, Cat. #9659, $25.00 – 30.00.

    "Hand" whiskey tumbler, $4.00 – 5.00.

Not shown:
    Cocktail shaker – $25.00 – 30.00.

"A VOTRE SANTE; SALUD; SKOL; TO YOUR HEALTH"
    Rooster, $6.00 – 8.00.

Not shown:
    Cocktail shaker, $30.00 – 35.00.

"PINKERSTEIN"
    This drink belongs to..., 4¹⁵⁄₁₆"h,
    $10.00 – 12.00.

HOLLAND HOUSE COCKTAIL MIX JIGGERS
    100 Pipers, 2½"h x 1¾"w, $3.00 – 4.00.

"GAY NINETIES WHISKEY BOTTLE SET"
    Gay Fad Studios Designs, Note: two styles of lettering,
    Decanter with stop (unmarked), $20.00 – 22.00.
    Whiskey tumbler, 4 oz., marked, $4.00 – 6.00.

Not shown:
    Rum decanter, $20.00 – 22.00.

WHISKEY TUMBLERS

"DUTCH"
"Tippsy," marked HA, 2⅞"h, 4 oz., **$6.00 – 8.00.**

"COACH"
Marked HA, 3⅛"h, 4 oz., **$6.00 – 8.00.**

"BICYCLE FOR FOUR"
Marked HA, 3⅛"h, 4 oz., **$6.00 – 8.00.**
Gay Fad Studios — part of Gay Nineties Design.

Not shown:
Cocktail shaker, **$25.00 – 30.00.**
Highball tumbler, **$5.00 – 6.00.**

"FROSTED APPLE BLOSSOM" – 2¹⁵⁄₁₆"h, **$4.00 – 5.00.**

"INDIAN" – Gay Fad Studios Designs, 4 oz.,
2¹⁵⁄₁₆"h, 1 oz. for squaw, 2 oz. for brave, 3 oz. for
medicine man, 4 oz. for happy hunting ground,
$6.00 – 8.00.

"TOTEM" – 4 oz., 2¹⁵⁄₁₆"h, 2 oz.,
"Low man on the totem pole," **$6.00 – 8.00.**

"COUNTRY MODERN"
Gay Fad Studios Design, 2⅞", **$6.00 – 8.00.**

Not shown:
80 oz. pitcher and tumbler set, **$60.00 – 65.00.**
"Square decorated" luncheon set of four, **$55.00 – 60.00.**
Batter set, Concentric Rings, **$50.00 – 60.00.**

"SAILOR"
4 oz., 2¹⁵⁄₁₆", "Down the hatch,"
1 oz. accordian, 2 oz. dance,
3 oz. fiddle, 4 oz. jump overboard,
$8.00 – 10.00.

WHISKEY TUMBLERS

"SAY WHEN" 4 OZ. HA TUMBLERS – Decorated by Gay Fad Studios Designs

"BOTTOMS UP"
   2¹⁵⁄₁₆"h, 1 oz. She Monkey, 2 oz. He Monkey, 3 oz. Monkey Shine, **$6.00 – 8.00.**

"SAY WHEN YOU-ALL"
   2¹⁵⁄₁₆"h, 1 oz. Yankees, 2 oz. Boll-Weevils, 3 oz. Carpetbaggers, To the Top - Rebels, **$6.00 – 8.00.**

"SAY WHEN (STEPS)"
   Hoover Dam, Nevada, 2¹⁵⁄₁₆", 0 for Rabbits, 1 oz. for Ladies, 2 oz. for Gentlemen, 3 oz. for Pigs, 4 oz. for Jackass, **$5.00 – 6.00.**

"SAY WHEN"
   Platonite, Hoover Dam, Nevada, souvenir, 2¾", **$6.00 – 8.00.**

"FOUNTAIN OF YOUTH"
   St. Augustine, Florida, 2⅞"h,
   Frosted, 4 oz., **$4.00 – 6.00.**

"BERMUDA ISLANDS"
   2⅞"h, 4 oz., **$5.00 – 7.00.**

"LADIES' DAY, MARCH 4"
   2⅞"h, frosted, **$6.00 – 8.00.**

"MY OLD KENTUCKY HOME SHRINE"
   Bardstown, Kentucky, 2⅞"h, 4 oz., frosted, **$4.00 – 6.00.**

"ABRAHAM LINCOLN NATIONAL HISTORICAL PARK" – Hodgenville, KY, 2⅞", 4 oz. , **$4.00 – 6.00.**

WHISKEY TUMBLERS

"KENTUCKY STATE PARKS"
Kentucky Dam/Kentucky Lake, 2⅞", 4 oz., **$4.00 – 6.00.**
Bluegrass State, 2⅞", 4 oz., **$4.00 – 6.00.**

"TEXAS" – "The Lone Star State," 2⅞", 4 oz., **$5.00 – 7.00.**

"NATIONAL BRIDGE - VIRGINIA"
Washington & Lee, 2⅞", 4 oz., **$4.00 – 6.00.**

"OLD MATT - OZARKS"
Shepherd of Hills, 2⅞", 4 oz., **$4.00 – 6.00.**

"HOT SPRINGS, ARKANSAS"
2⅞", 4 oz., **$4.00 – 6.00.**

"NATIONAL CAPITOL AT WASHINGTON"
2⅞", 4 oz., **$4.00 – 6.00.**

BATTERY JARS

"BATTERY JARS"
One of Hazel-Atlas' earlier big selling products
was battery jars of the type depicted in this
1928 Sears catalog. **$25.00 – 30.00.**

GOBLETS

These represent the type of tableware goblets that were being produced in the 1960s. They were a little more elegant than your average tumbler. Indeed, in a 60s catalog of Continental Can's that was geared toward the 1970s market, there was a heading: "Shapes mean more to a woman." Obviously, there was a greater emphasis on pleasing designs during this era, evidenced by the signed wares that began to appear. Designs by artists began to carry their names on the glass. In additon, the 1960s heralded the "reign of Camelot" and the White House first lady, Jacqueline Kennedy, who was bringing style to the old capital. Word was that she was appalled at the condition of the White House and was determined about refurbishing it! The nation took pride and interest in what she wore, what glassware she chose for the nation's table ("The President's House," line #7780; by Morgantown), her hairstyle, and her jewelry (famous pearls). She got almost as much press coverage as the President. In short, her elegance and style was translated to the marketplace and thus, the nation at large. The blue and crystal Capri stems with their hexagon feet are reminiscent of Colonial styles while the indented crinolined effect of Moroccan amethyst wares lent a bejeweled and tactile charm to everyday wares. Capri and Moroccan tableware can be found in the Pattern section in the back of the book.

"MOROCCAN AMETHYST CRINOLINE"
Tumbler, $9.00 – 11.00.
Tea, $9.00 – 11.00.
Juice, $8.00 – 10.00.

WHITE WARE "CRINOLINE"
Sherbet, $2.00 – 3.00.
Tea, $3.00 – 4.00.

CRYSTAL "CRINOLINE"
Juice, $2.00 – 3.00.

FLASHED "CRINOLINE"
Pail, $8.00 – 10.00.

"CAPRI HEXAGON SHERBET" – $6.00 – 8.00.

"CAPRI HEXAGON WATER" – $8.00 – 10.00.

"CRYSTAL HEXAGON WATER" – $3.00 – 4.00.

MUGS – COFFEE & SHAVING

Over the course of Hazel wares' history, their white products were advertised first as Opal, then Platonite, Opaque, Whiteware, and Milk White. It is said the first Opal ware had a translucence at the edge that by the 1930s Platonite times had settled into a purer white. Below are mugs from various time periods. Although connoisieurs claim to tell differences, the catalogs themselves were a bit muddy on which was what. All these mugs are marked HA.

"COFFEE TIME" LANDMARK COMPANY LOGO
Cat. #0625, Platonite coffee mug,
9⅛" oz., 3½"h x 3¼"w at top, **$10.00 – 12.00.**

"OPAL ROSE"
1930s painted shaving mug, with loop
handle, rim foot, and flair rim, **$25.00 – 30.00.**

"PLATONITE HANDLED MUG"
1940s/1950s, 3½"h x 4²⁷⁄₆₄"w, Cat. #0-989.
You will notice the catalog number calls
this "opal," but it's advertised on a catalog
(see pg. 157) headed "Platonite," **$10.00 – 12.00.**

"PLATONITE COFFEE MUG"
Cat. #0625, 9⅛" oz., 3½"h x
3¼"w at top, **$10.00 – 12.00.**

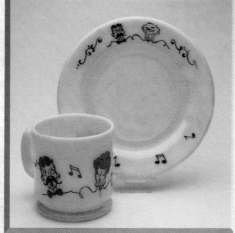

"GAY NINETIES" - COUPLE & DAD
Possibly Gay Fad Studios Gay Nineties Series. 1950s, Cat. #0-989. 1950s saw a great marketing of all things from what was then termed the "Gay Nineties" period of history.
Mug, **$15.00 – 20.00.**
Plate, **$10.00 – 12.00.**
A "Pappy" mug has also been seen.

"RED MAPLE LEAF"
Cat. #0-59, mid-1950s, called "Milk" mug of the late 1930s/early 1940s, geared toward children and now part of Red Maple Leaf wares marketed to grown-ups for coffee and cereal, **$12.00 – 15.00.**

FRONT   BACK

"SANTA SOUVENIR MUG"
Cat #0-59, advertising lunch at Crowley's, **$35.00 – 40.00.**

FRONT

BACK

"BOTTOMS UP" – Niagra Falls souvenir mug, **$12.00 – 15.00.**

"RED ROOSTER COFFEE MUG"
Late 1950s, Cat. #W587, indicating Whiteware, **$12.00 – 14.00.**

"DIXIE SOUVENIR MUG"
Advertising the flag and the song; probably from late 1950s/early 1960s when Civil Rights was a national sore spot, particularly in the South. This proclaims "Southland Forever" and would have been the less subtle way of stating sides while drinking your coffee and reading the newspaper. **$20.00 – 25.00.**

MUGS – LARGE

FRONT

FINGERGRIP HANDLES AND CONCENTRIC RINGS ON BOTTOMS
Cat. # 228
4⅞"h x 3⅛"w, 16 oz., $10.00 – 12.00 each.

"OLD GRAY MARE"
"HOW DRY I AM"
"YOU TELL ME YOUR DREAMS"
"THE BAND PLAYED ON"

Not shown:
Milk pitcher, wih spout, of like design,
Cat. #290, 16 oz., $22.00 – 25.00.

BACK

GAY NINETIES MUG
Gay Fad Studios Designs,
$10.00 – 12.00.

"BUCKEYE STATE, OHIO"
Fingergrip handle and
Concentric Rings on bottom,
4⅞"h x 3⅛"w, $12.00 – 14.00.

TOASTING BEER MUGS ON FROSTED GLASS
All Gay Fad Studios Designs. Ten of 12 available shown here. All marked HA.

"GERMANY," "ENGLAND, " "FRANCE"
  $15.00 – 20.00 each.
"USA" – $20.00 – 25.00.
"SPAIN" – $15.00 – 20.00.

"SWEDEN"
$15.00 – 20.00.

"FINLAND," "MEXICO, CACTUS"
"MEXICO, SALUD," "POLAND"
  $15.00 – 20.00 each.

PITCHERS – CREAM & MILK

"CHEVRON"
Sugar, 3", Ritz, $15.00 – 20.00.
Milk, 3¾", Ritz, $20.00 – 25.00.
Creamer, 3", Ritz, $15.00 – 20.00.
Milk, 3¾", crystal, $8.00 – 10.00.

Not shown:
Milk, 3¾", pink, $25.00 – 30.00 (rare).

"LITTLE DEB" – Lemonade server set #207, Northwestern Products Co., combinaton of cream pitcher and Moderntone shot tumblers. $55.00 – 75.00 in box.

"GAY RAINBOW"
$6.00 – 8.00 each.
Display ad, $15.00 – 20.00.

JUICE PITCHERS

We believe this page graphically represents what the industry calls a "marriage." The pitchers appear to be Federal Glass Company's products (#180 – round; #2604 – square). However, the juice glasses are clearly marked HA. This happened when a decorating company painted the designs and mixed various company wares together to suit their needs. It's a common occurrence with hand-decorated wares. Usually the "set" is identified with whatever marking prevails.

"IVY" SET
Gay Fad Studios Design, came both frosted and clear.
Pitcher, Federal's 32 oz., no mark, #180, $15.00 – 20.00.
Tumbler, marked HA, 2⅞"h x 2⁄₁₆"w, $4.00 – 5.00.

ORIGINAL SET CAME WITH PITCHER AND SIX 4 OZ. TUMBLERS.

PALM TREE SET
Gay Fad Studios Designs
Pitcher, Federal's #2640, no mark, 36 oz.,
frosted, $25.00 – 30.00.
Tumbler, 2⅞"h x 2⁄₁₆"w, $4.00 – 5.00.

Not shown:
Batter pitcher set, with syrup, c. 1954, $55.00 – 60.00.

"FLORAL LEAVES" SET
Pitcher, Cat. #209, 38 oz., $25.00 – 30.00.
Tumbler, $6.00 – 8.00.

SEE MATCHING TUMBLER ON PAGE 22.

"DOGWOOD CHAIN" SET
Pitcher with black, Cat. #209, 38 oz., $25.00 – 30.00.
Pitcher with white, Cat. #209, 38 oz., $28.00 – 30.00.
Tumbler with black, $6.00 – 8.00.
Tumbler with white, $7.00 – 9.00.

SEE CONCENTRIC RINGS 80 OZ. PITCHER ON PAGE 38.

JUICE TUMBLERS

"HORIZONTAL RIB"
"Double cup" (juice or egg), Cat. #167,
4¾ oz., 4¹³⁄₃₂"h, $8.00 – 10.00.

"GOOD MORNING"
Juice (or egg) cup, $12.00 – 15.00.

"STARS" – 3¹¹⁄₁₆", $6.00 – 8.00.
"COSMOS" – 3¹¹⁄₁₆", $6.00 – 8.00.

"SEASON'S GREETINGS"
Gay Fad Studios Designs
5 oz., 3½" x 2⅜", $18.00 – 20.00.

"VERTICAL STRIPES"
Gay Fad Studios Designs
2⅞"h, $4.00 – 5.00.

"STRIPES" – 4 oz., $4.00 – 5.00.
"TOMATOES" – 4 oz., $5.00 – 6.00.

JUICE BOTTLES

We know Libbey called their like ware "Handeservers," that Hocking called theirs "Juice Chillers, and that Federal advertised "Handi-Serv Decanters." However, we were unable to locate a source that would tell us if Hazel-Atlas had a special name for their plastic cap, refrigerator juice bottles. Hazel-Atlas juice bottles are characterized by Concentric Rings on bottle neck and on bottom of bottle. If you know, we'd appreciate a postcard or e-mail at GFlore@aol.com — as well as any other helpful Hazel-Atlas tidbits! It is possible that these long-ago plastic lids may be almost as valuable as the container itself!

"COCKS-CROW"
Cocktail juice tumbler, $6.00 – 8.00.
Ice/mixing bowl, Cat. #0-774,
2 7/8"h x 6"w, $20.00 – 22.00.
Juice bottle, Concentric Rings,
7 7/8", $15.00 – 20.00.

"GAZELLE"
Plastic top missing, 7 7/8", $15.00 – 20.00.
Tumblers, 8 oz., shell, no mark,
5 1/16", sham (heavy) bottom, $4.00 – 6.00 each.

JUICE/MILK BOTTLE – 34 oz., 7 3/4", Cat. #5113, juice with fruit embossed on one side; milk on other side. Ribbed middle with pebble finish, came with standard red, green, or yellow lid, $8.00 – 10.00.

"ORANGES"
Juice bottle, Concentric Rings, 7 7/8",
Marked HA-K4, $15.00 – 18.00.

JUICE BOTTLES

"ORANGE/TOMATO"
Concentric rings juice bottle, marked HAK23
(old design; used in pitcher type beverage sets of mid-1930s.)
7⅞", **$15.00 – 18.00.**
Juice tumblers, unmarked, 3⁹⁄₁₆", **$4.00 – 5.00 each.**

"WHITE WHEAT WITH GOLD FENCING"
Concentric Rings juice bottle, 7⅞", **$8.00 – 10.00.**
Marked HA, **$12.00 – 13.00.**

"THREE STRIPE"
Representing milk, orange, or tomato
Juice, Concentric Rings juice bottle,
Marked HA-K2-7, 7⅞", **$12.00 – 15.00.**

PITCHERS – MILK

Notice that these 19½ oz. pitchers come in two styles, one with a flat rim with the spout below the rim, and one with a raised spout. The flat-rimmed version has been found with a metal beater top, leading to the conclusion that these were marketed as an early whipped cream or egg/eggnog whipping type product. At any rate, we know these were among the first greenware products offered in the 1930s catalog of kitchenware items. They were Catalog #3027 and collectors of "Ribbon" pattern items often include them with their sets since the design is similar. Without the raised lip they measure 5" tall.

SEE "COLONIAL COUPLE" PATTERN, PAGE 155 FOR
ANOTHER EXAMPLE OF THESE TYPE OF PITCHERS.

DOTS
Red trim, Platonite, 5", **$45.00 – 55.00.**

COBALT
Flat rim, 5", **$85.00 – 100.00.**

PITCHERS – MILK

GREEN – Flat rim, Cat. #3027, 5", **$25.00 – 30.00.**
OPAL – Raised spout, marked HA, 5", **$15.00 – 20.00.**

PINK – Flashed color over Platonite,
$18.00 – 22.00.

#9870 "VERTICAL RIB" PITCHER
  Matches #9869, 9 oz. tumbler.
Crystal
  80 oz. pitcher, **$20.00 – 25.00.**
  Shakers **$5.00 each.**

Not shown:
  9 oz. tumbler, **$4.00 – 6.00.**

Also available in
Amethyst (rare)
  80 oz. pitcher, **$45.00 – 50.00.**
  9 oz. tumbler, **$9.00 – 11.00.**
Pink
  80 oz. pitcher, **$25.00 – 30.00.**
  9 oz. tumbler, **$6.00 – 8.00.**

PITCHER SETS – CONCENTRIC RINGS

"DUTCH TULIP"
  Concentric Rings blank, Cat. #9908.

  CRYSTAL WITH BLUE
    80 oz. pitcher, **$35.00 – 40.00.**

Not shown:
  9 oz. tumbler, **$8.00 – 10.00.**

  RITZ WITH WHITE
    80 oz. pitcher, **$75.00 – 80.00.**

Not shown:
  9 oz. tumbler, **$15.00 – 18.00.**

PITCHER SETS – CONCENTRIC RINGS

"DELICIOUS FRUIT"
Concentric Rings blank, Cat. #9908.
Pitcher, 9⅜"h, $25.00 – 30.00.
Tumbler, 5¹⁄₁₆"h, $6.00 – 8.00; in original box, $95.00.

"DOTS"
Concentric Rings blank, Cat. #9908.
Pitcher, 9⅜"h, $30.00 – 35.00.
Tumbler, 5¹⁄₁₆"h, $8.00 – 10.00.

"PETUNIA"
Concentric Rings blank, Cat. #9908.
Pitcher, 9⅜"h, $25.00 – 30.00.

Not shown:
Tumbler, 5", $8.00 – 10.00.

"FIESTA STRIPE"
Concentric Rings blank, Cat. #9908.
Pitcher, 9⅜"h, $25.00 – 30.00.

Not shown:
Tumbler, 5", $8.00 – 10.00.

"DOGWOOD CHAIN"
Pitcher, 9⅜"h, $30.00 – 35.00.
Tumbler (shown on pg. 33), 5", $8.00 – 10.00.

FRONT   BACK

MEXICAN SCENE
Decoration #1166 (blue, orange, red, white, yellow).
9 oz. water tumbler, $8.00 – 10.00.

Not shown:
Pitcher, 80 oz., 9½"h, $40.00 – 45.00.
12 oz. tea tumbler, $12.00 – 15.00.
9 oz. tall water tumbler, $8.00 – 10.00.
5 oz. fruit tumbler, $8.00 – 10.00.

PITCHER SETS – CONCENTRIC RINGS

"ROOSTER IN IVY"
Pitcher, 9⅜"h, $35.00 – 40.00.

Not shown:
Tumbler, 5", $10.00 – 12.00.

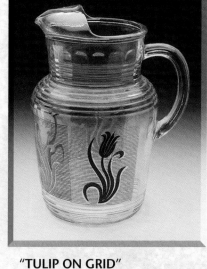

"TULIP ON GRID"
Pitcher, 9⅜"h, $25.00 – 30.00.

Not shown:
Tumbler, 5", $6.00 – 8.00.
Turquoise and red.

"BLUEBIRD DECORATION"
Tumbler, 5", $6.00 – 8.00.
Pitcher, 9⅜"h, $35.00 – 40.00.

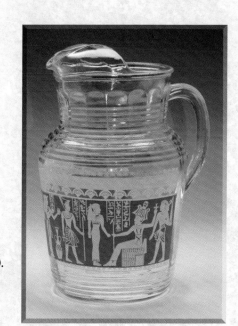

"WEDGWOOD BLUE"
Egyptian design
Pitcher, 9⅜"h, $25.00 – 30.00.

Not shown:
Tumbler, 5", $6.00 – 8.00.

SEE PAGE 214 FOR EXAMPLES OF BOTH STYLES OF "SHIPS" PITCHERS.

PITCHER SETS – WITH OPTIC

These optic style pitchers appear to have spanned the mid-1930s to 1940s; after the 1940s, they appear to have featured mostly the Concentric Rings blank in their pitcher sets.

COLORED SPIRAL
Decoration #450 red and white on Ritz Blue.
Also came in red and white on crystal, yellow, white, and blue, and white on crystal.
Tumbler, 9 oz., tall table, 4½", **$12.00 – 15.00.**

Not shown:
Pitcher, 80 oz., with ice lip, 9⅜", **$50.00 – 55.00.**
Tumbler, 9 oz., table, 3⅜", **$12.00 – 15.00.**
Tumbler, 5 oz., juice, 3¾", **$10.00 – 12.00.**

"ASTER"
Cat. #1816, with ice lip.
Green, 80 oz., **$50.00 – 60.00.**
Tumbler, tea, 5", **$10.00 – 12.00.**

RHUMBA
Cat. #1816, black, green, and red on crystal,
and Ritz Blue with white,
60 oz., with ice lip, **$50.00 – 55.00.**
9 oz. tall table (highball), **$10.00 – 12.00.**

Not shown:
44 oz. ice tub, **$50.00 – 55.00.**
12 oz. tea, **$12.00 – 15.00.**
9 oz. table, **$8.00 – 10.00.**
5 oz. fruit, **$6.00 – 8.00.**

"SUNRISE/SUNSET"
Decoration #1154, Cat. #1816,
Colors: yellow, blue, green, and red.
Tumbler, 9 oz. tall drinks (highball), **$8.00 – 10.00.**
Pitcher, 80 oz., with ice lip, **$30.00 – 35.00.**

Not shown:
Tumbler, 12 oz. tea, **$10.00 – 12.00.**
Tumbler, 9 oz. table, **$8.00 – 10.00.**
Tumbler, 5 oz. juice, **$8.00 – 10.00.**

FINE RIB ITEMS

FINE RIB ITEMS HAVE BEEN VERY POPULAR WITH COLLECTORS FOR 30 YEARS.

MARMALADE
Without metal slotted top,
Ritz Blue, $20.00 – 22.00.

20 OZ. MILK PITCHER
Cat. #9891.
Flashed color, $20.00 – 25.00.

Not shown:
Crystal, $8.00 – 10.00.
Pink, $15.00 – 20.00.

VERTICAL RIB
Shot tumbler, unmarked, traditionally ascribed to Hazel-Atlas (who did make a bulged top tumbler and was fond of ribs and concentric circle designs in its wares), $8.00 – 12.00.

Not shown:
Tiny Tilt pitcher – Should accompany
Rib shot tumbler, very rare, $110.00 – 125.00.

80 OZ. TILT PITCHER
With ice lip, blown, Cat. #9932.
Ritz Blue, $55.00 – 75.00.

Not shown:
Crystal, $20.00 – 25.00.
Pink, $45.00 – 55.00.
Flashed color, pink, $40.00 – 45.00.

"ROLY POLY" – $40.00 – 45.00.

TUMBLERS

Cat. #		CRYSTAL	PINK	RITZ BLUE	FLASHED COLORS
9937	5 oz., flat juice	$3.00 – 4.00	$10.00 – 12.00	$14.00 – 16.00	$8.00 – 10.00
9939	9 oz., table	$5.00 – 6.00	$8.00 – 10.00	$12.00 – 14.00	$10.00 – 12.00
9940	12 oz., tea	$6.00 – 8.00	$12.00 – 14.00	$18.00 – 20.00	$10.00 – 12.00

JUICE PITCHER

Cat. #		CRYSTAL	PINK	RITZ BLUE	FLASHED COLORS
9937	24 oz., juice	$10.00 – 12.00	$30.00 – 35.00	$50.00 – 55.00	$30.00 – 35.00

PITCHERS – VARIOUS STYLES

COLONIAL FOOTED PITCHER
With thumb-rest handle, 6½" x 5⅜".
Crystal, **$15.00 – 18.00**.

Not shown:
Green, **$30.00 – 35.00**.

RIM FOOTED PITCHER
41 oz., Cat. #3026.
Crystal, **$28.00 – 33.00**.

Not shown:
Green, **$35.00 – 40.00**.

Also available:
Matching footed tea.
Crystal, **$4.00 – 5.00**.
Green, **$8.00 – 10.00**.

PUNCH, EGGNOG, & TOM AND JERRY SETS

In the late 1940s and early 1950s there was a trend in the glass industry to feature what were then termed "milk glass" products. Most of these sets date from that time frame. There was an abundance of "party" type items being produced, trays, buffet servers, lazy susans, and bridge and punch sets, which indicates there was an eagerness to congregate with friends, perhaps a result of the euphoria of WWII being behind them. In the case of eggnog sets, there was a long-standing tradition of serving eggnog at Christmas. We saw one 1949 advertisement for the "Top Hat" one stating it to be the "ever famous Hazel-Atlas punch/eggnog set," indicating it must have been a product for a while. For those curious types, like me, the term "Tom and Jerry" supposedly came to us from a famous English Pub, run by Tom and Jerry, where one could sit and talk with friends and enjoy a good mug of ale. Thus, "Tom and Jerry" type mugs.

"AULD LANG SYNE"
Punch cup, Cat. #0-59, 3", **$3.00 – 4.00**.

Not shown:
Punch bowl, Cat. #0-777, 9" diam., **$15.00 – 20.00**.

CHRISTMAS CHEER "TOM AND JERRY"
Sometimes referred to as "Top Hat."
Punch bowl, Cat. #0-777, 9" diam., **$15.00 – 20.00**.
Punch cup, Cat. #0-59, 3" (2⅞" actually), **$3.00 – 4.00 each**.

PUNCH, EGGNOG, & TOM AND JERRY SETS

"COLONIAL"
Indented bottom.
Punch bowl, 5¾"h x 9¾"w, **$15.00 – 20.00.**
Punch cup, 3⅛"h, **$3.00 – 4.00.**

"COLONIAL"
Eggnog cup, Cat #0-59, 3", **$4.00 – 5.00.**

Not shown:
Eggnog bowl, Cat. #0-777, 9" diam., **$20.00 – 25.00.**

"CURRIER & IVES"
Chopping ice scene.
Punch cup, Cat. #0-59, 3", **$4.00 – 5.00.**

Not shown:
Punch bowl , Cat. #0-777, 9" diam., **$20.00 – 25.00.**

"DOTS" ("BALLOONS") – This same design was used in a 1938 multicolored beverage set called Carnival. However, the colors used were green, orange, red, and white. They did refer to the dots in their ad as "balloons." They are definitely suggestive of a party! Punch bowl, indented bottom, 5¾"h x 9¾"w, **$25.00 – 30.00**; punch cups, **$4.00 – 5.00 each.**

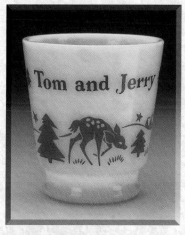

"DEER SCENE"
Indented bottom.
Punch cup, 3⅛"h, **$3.00 – 4.00.**

Not shown:
Punch bowl, 5¾"h x 9¾"w, **$20.00 – 25.00.**

PUNCH, EGGNOG, & TOM AND JERRY SETS

"JINGLE BELLS"
Punch bowl, Cat. #0-777, 9" diam., **$15.00 – 20.00.**
Punch cups, Cat. #0-595, **$3.00 – 4.00 each.**

"FESTIVE"
Gay Fad Studios Designs
Eggnog bowl, Cat. #0-777, 9" diam., **$20.00 – 25.00.**
Eggnog cup, Cat. #0-59, **$4.00 – 5.00 each.**

WILLIAMSPORT or **WILLIAMSBURG** – Cat. #8866.
We mention this 1970 version punch set here because it was advertised in the Hazelware catalog as Williamsport. However, it came in a box labeled "Williamsburg," with the same item number. It cost $3.00 back then, complete with plastic ladel and hooks for 12 cups. Even though the Hazel-Atlas Company sold in 1956, their product lines were still cataloged as late as 1970 as Hazelware products.
Punch cup, Cat. #747, 6 oz., sq., **$2.00 – 3.00.**

Not shown:
Punch bowl, 6½ qt., sq., **$10.00 – 12.00.**

TUMBLERS – ANIMALS

Although Cathy purchased the Derby Winners packaged as a giftset in the mid-1950s, we've encountered many stories while doing this book saying these type tumblers were also used as packaging for diverse items, i.e. cottage cheese, sour cream, peanut butter, and jellies; and since "Packer Tumblers" were a big part of the Hazel-Atlas business from the early 1900s, there's no reason to believe these were not used as such. Indeed, people were absolutely euphoric sometime around WWI over a new Anchor lid that allowed them to machine close a top with an air-tight seal on the side of a container, thereby greatly increasing their Packer Tumbler business!

BIRDS – Goldfinch, 5"h, Cardinal, 5"h, Oriole, 5"h, Bluebird, 5"h; all with two views, **$5.00 – 6.00 each.**

BUDGIES PARAKEETS – 3½"h.
Red, juice, **$6.00 – 8.00.**
Blue, juice, **$6.00 – 8.00.**

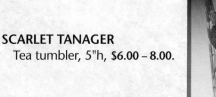

SCARLET TANAGER
Tea tumbler, 5"h, **$6.00 – 8.00.**

DERBY WINNING HORSES – 5½"h, Ponder, '49; Middleground, '50; Count Turf, '51; Hill Gail, '52; Dark Star, '53; Determined, '54. **$25.00 – 30.00 each.**

TUMBLERS – ANIMALS

DEER
Possibly for Christmas trade.
$8.00 – 10.00.

SCOTTIES
Double rim lip red juice.
$12.00 – 15.00.

SPLIT RAIL FENCE FOX
One in a series of different animals,
5"h x 2⅞"w, **$11.00 – 14.00.**

PICKET FENCE COCKER SPANIELS
One in a series of different colored
Cockers, (i.e. blue, yellow, black),
5⁵⁄₁₆"h, **$12.00 – 15.00.**

SCOTTIES WITH PURINA BASE
3½"h, rim lip, red, blue on
crystal, **$12.00 – 15.00.**

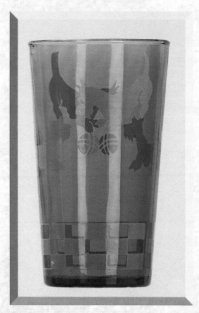

SCOTTIES WITH PURINA BASE
White on Ritz Blue, **$20.00 – 25.00.**

Household Table Tumblers— Juice Tumblers—Miniature Mug by HAZEL-ATLAS

389–8 oz. Table Tumbler
Light Weight
Pkd. 6 doz. ctn. Wt. 30 lbs.
Height 4⅛" Top 2⅞" Base 2¼₆"

660–8 oz. Table Tumbler
Light Weight
Pkd. 6 doz. ctn. Wt. 30 lbs.
Height 3⅝" Top 2⅞" Base 2¼₆"

372–9 oz. Table Tumbler
Light Weight
Pkd. 6 doz. ctn. Wt. 32 lbs.
Height 4¼₂" Top 2⅞" Base 2¼"

1054–9 oz. Table Tumbler
Sq. Bottom—Light Weight
Pkd. 6 doz. ctn. Wt. 29 lbs.
Height 4¼₆" Top 2²⁵⁄₃₂" Base 2¼₆"

1214–9 oz. Table Tumbler
Light Weight
Pkd. 6 doz. ctn. Wt. 29 lbs.
Height 4⅛" Top 3³⁄₃₂" Base 2⁵⁄₃₂"

1229–9 oz. Table Tumbler
Light Weight
Pkd. 6 doz. ctn. Wt. 29 lbs.
Height 3⅞" Top 2¹¹⁄₁₆" Base 2½"

1261 (†1261 H-S)–9 oz. Table Tumbler
Light Weight
Pkd. 6 doz. ctn. Wt. 28 lbs.
Height 3¾" Top 3" Base 2¹¹⁄₃₂"

1564–9 oz. Table Tumbler
Light Weight
Pkd. 6 doz. ctn. Wt. 29 lbs.
Height 4⅛" Top 2⅞" Base 2⁷⁄₃₂"

9625–9½ oz. Table Tumbler
Light Weight
Pkd. 6 doz. ctn. Wt. 28 lbs.
Height 4⁵⁄₃₂" Top 2⅞" Base 2"

1709–9 oz. Table Tumbler
Light Weight
Pkd. 6 doz. ctn. Wt. 30 lbs.
Height 4⅛" Top 2⅞" Base 2⁷⁄₃₂"

9601–9 oz. Table Tumbler
Light Weight
Pkd. 6 doz. ctn. Wt. 30 lbs.
Height 4¼" Top 3⁷⁄₃₂" Base 2³⁄₁₆"

523–9 oz. Table Tumbler
Light Weight
Pkd. 6 doz. ctn. Wt. 32 lbs.
Height 4" Top 3¼" Base 2¼"

371–5 oz. Small Tumbler
Fruit Juice
Pkd. 6 doz. ctn. Wt. 21 lbs.
Height 3¹¹⁄₁₆" Top 2⁵⁄₁₆" Base 1²⁵⁄₃₂"

1220–5 oz. Small Tumbler
Fruit Juice
Pkd. 6 doz. ctn. Wt. 23 lbs.
Height 3⅞" Top 2¹⁹⁄₃₂" Base 1¾"

1290–5 oz. Small Tumbler
Square Bottom—Fruit Juice
Pkd. 6 doz. ctn. Wt. 21 lbs.
Height 3¹⁵⁄₃₂" Top 2⅜" Base 1¹¹⁄₁₆"

169–1¾ oz. Mug
Miniature Barrel
Pkd. 6 doz. ctn. Wt. 20 lbs.
Height 2¹⁵⁄₃₂" Top 2" Base 1⁷⁄₁₆"

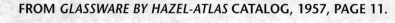

†Item numbers within ( ) in light face type are the former numbers

FROM *GLASSWARE BY HAZEL-ATLAS* CATALOG, 1957, PAGE 11.

TUMBLERS – HOUSEHOLD

14 OPTIC
Pink, 3¼", **$4.00 – 5.00**.
Crystal, 3⁹⁄₁₆", **$2.00 – 3.00**.

CRYSTAL AND PINK WITH OPTICS
Pink tumbler, 4⅛", 30 optic, **$4.00 – 5.00**.
Bowl, 1½"h x 4"w, 34 optic, c. 1924, **$3.00 – 4.00**.
Shot, 12-panel indented bottom, 36 optic top, **$2.00 – 3.00**.
Crystal with red tulip, 4¹³⁄₁₆"h, 28 optic, **$4.00 – 5.00**.

TUMBLERS
CLEAR

Pressed clear glass; bell shape; spiral fluted; medium weight. Capacity, 9 ounces.

No.	Per Doz.	Per Gross
1552	$0.35	$3.60

One gross in carton
Weight, Per Gross, 63 lbs.

HORSE SHOE BOTTOM

Pressed clear glass; with horse shoe design. Medium weight. Capacity, 9 ounces.

No.	Per Doz.	Per Gross
122½	$0.35	$3.60

One gross in carton
Weight, Per Gross, 63 lbs.

LUCKY 3 TUMBLER ASSORTMENT
CONTAINS

4 Doz. Crystal Tumblers
4 Doz. Green Tumblers
4 Doz. Rose Tumblers

Per assortment **$3.60**
This assortment gives you three different colors of tumblers at the carton lot price.

ADVERTISEMENT FROM 1937
LOUISVILLE STOVE COMPANY, PAGE 52.

SEE PAGE 142 FOR OPAL VASE WITH RUFFLED TOP.

CRYSTAL
#311, c. 1940s, patterned, footed, bulbous middle, flared rim prolifically dispersed in crystal, **$6.00 – 8.00**.

Not shown:
Pink, **$15.00 – 20.00** (rare).

COLA FOUNTAIN LINE #394
4 oz. with punty indents, 4⅛". **$8.00 – 10.00** each. This came with straight or cupped rim in 4, 6, 7, 8, 10, and 12 oz. sizes, and will increase values **$1.00** an ounce. Some had a cola syrup line about an inch from the bottom. These will bring **$2.00 – 3.00** more.

TUMBLERS – HOUSEHOLD

DUTCH TULIP
4½"h x 2¹¹⁄₁₆"w,
Crystal, $15.00 – 18.00.

Not shown:
Ritz Blue with white, $20.00 – 25.00 each.

FLASHED COLORS
Burgundy, 4⅜", $8.00 – 10.00.
Aqua fingerhold, 3⅞", $6.00 – 8.00.

28 OPTIC SWIRL
4"h x 2¾"w, $6.00 – 8.00

COLORS – These bold multicolored 1940s wares probably had names, but we couldn't locate any information on what they originally were. So, in order to facilitate a uniformity of understanding of what is being discussed, we've taken the liberty of placing names on these within quote marks, trying to hold onto the design element in some fashion. Please understand tumblers were one of Hazel-Atlas's main products for 50 years. So, there should be hundreds of thousands, perhaps millions of these out there still. Many of the earlier products carry their logo of "H" over "A." However, it appeared that as time went on, more and more companies didn't want Hazel-Atlas assigning their logo to their products; so many are unmarked, though made by Hazel-Atlas. If you have product information of any kind on these wares, please let us know.

"CHINESE PUZZLE"
Tumbler – $5.00 – 6.00.

Not shown:
Ice bowl – $20.00 – 25.00.

"RICK RACK"
4½", $5.00 – 6.00.
Probably part of 7 pc.
pitcher and tumbler set.

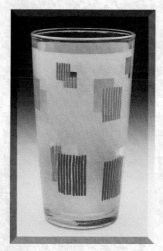

"SHADOW BOXES" – $5.00 – 6.00.

– 49 –

TUMBLERS – HOUSEHOLD

"FESTIVE GLASSES" – Original Hazelware packaged set of four, 6 oz., juice, **$25.00.**

"RED STRIPE GLASSES"
Set with rack, **$35.00 – 40.00.**

"GOTHIC BEVERAGE GLASSES"
Cat. #B-77, Capri Blue, 6½" oz., **$6.00 – 7.00.**
3⅛", 5 oz., **$6.00 – 7.00.**
4¼", 9 oz., **$7.00 – 8.00.**
5", 12 oz., **$9.00 – 11.00.**
Boxed dozen, **$75.00 – 85.00.**

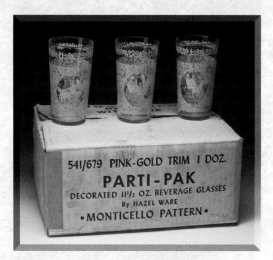

"MONTICELLO PATTERN"
Cat. #54, tumbler, 11½ oz., **$2.00 – 3.00.**
1 dozen "parti-pak" boxed set, **$35.00 – 40.00.**

"PLATONITE"
Tumbler, 5¹⁄₁₆", Fleur de Lis, **$8.00 – 9.00.**
Tumblers, 5¹⁄₁₆", Mocha Chocolate (with matching plate) or Platonite, **$4.00 – 5.00 each.**

"PLATONITE CURRIER & IVES"
Tumbler, 5¹⁄₁₆", **$8.00 – 10.00 each.**

TUMBLERS – HOUSEHOLD

STRAIGHT SHELL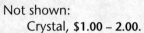
Cat. #9592, 5 oz., Bead Edge.
Cobalt, **$12.00 – 15.00.**

Not shown:
Crystal, **$1.00 – 2.00.**

"ANTIQUE" – 5⅛", 2¹⁵⁄₁₆"h,
no mark, **$6.00 – 8.00.**

"NEWPORT" – **$40.00 – 50.00.**

SEE NEWPORT PATTERN
ON PAGE 190.

"BARREL"
Hotel tumbler, Cat. #376.
Green, 9 oz., **$5.00 – 6.00.**

Not shown:
Crystal, **$2.00 – 3.00.**
Cobalt, **$10.00 – 12.00.**
Pink, **$6.00 – 8.00.**

SPIRAL FLUTE
9 oz. table tumblers, 4⅛"h x 2⅞",
Cat. #1552.
Pink, **$8.00 – 10.00**
Green, **$8.00 – 10.00.**

Not shown:
Blue, **$10.00 – 12.00**
Crystal, **$5.00 – 6.00.**

"STACKED PANEL"
Cobalt, **$12.00 – 15.00.**

Not shown:
Amethyst, **$8.00 – 10.00.**

TUMBLERS – PRODUCT PACKAGING

We have put in the colors we have seen. There are very possibly more colors in these designs as will be indicated by the dots afterward. Also, if we know at least one of the products packaged in these, that will be indicated in parentheses.

FLORALS & FRUIT (ADD $2.00 – 3.00 FOR LABELS OR LIDS)

"IVY"
Sour cream, 5⅞"h, green, pink...,
$5.00 – 7.00.

"PICKET FENCE ORCHID"
5¼", Blue Plate Strawberry Preserves, blue, pink, or yellow...,
$10.00 – 12.00 each.

"DAHLIA"
5⅞"h, "½ pint liq."
in design at bottom,
yellow, green, red..., **$6.00 – 8.00.**

"WHEAT SHEAVES"
Refrigerator jar, with lid, 3½"h,
Penn. Maid Sour Cream, **$8.00 – 10.00.**
Tumbler, 5⅞"h, **$5.00 – 7.00.**
May have held cottage cheese.

"POMEGRANATE"
4½"h, Cahill's fruit jelly, **$10.00 – 12.00.**
Specific advertising wares are
collectible in themselves.

"JELLY GLASS LIDS" – With HA embossing, 3⅜" and 2¾". Since these lids have no sealing rings inside, we believe they may be earlier type lids which mostly just covered the tops of the jelly jars, rather than sealing them. They sometimes had a paper permeated in sulphur between the lid & contents as a preservation measure. **$5.00 – 6.00 each.**

– 52 –

TUMBLERS – PRODUCT PACKAGING
OBJECTS

"EIFFEL TOWER"
$6.00 – 8.00.

"WHITE SHIPS"
18 panel optic, $8.00 – 10.00.
Two scenes of one glass shown.

"YOUR HOME IS YOUR CASTLE"
6⁷⁄₁₆"h x 3"w, $8.00 – 10.00.

TRANSPORTATION

"RED/BLACK, WHITE BUGGY/CAR"
5⅝", Scroll borders with both sides
shown. $6.00 – 8.00.

"GREEN CAR"
Ribbed bottom tumblers, 6", $6.00 – 8.00.
"YELLOW BUGGY" – 4½", $4.00 – 5.00.

SCROLL BORDERS:
"GREEN/BLACK BICYCLE"
4⅞", Jewel Tea Jelly, $8.00 – 10.00.
"RED/BLUE ROADSTER"
4½", $6.00 – 8.00.

SCROLL HORSE AND HORSELESS CARRIAGE
Cocktail shaker, $20.00 – 25.00.
4 oz. tumblers, $5.00 – 6.00 each.

TUMBLERS – PRODUCT PACKAGING
PEOPLE & CHARACTERS

ABRAHAM LINCOLN – 5½", #2 Series, $10.00 – 12.00.
ROBERT E. LEE – 5½", #4, $10.00 – 12.00.

RIM LIP STATESMEN SERIES:
 Thomas Jefferson, **$8.00 – 10.00.**
 Daniel Webster, **$8.00 – 10.00.**
Also found with Abraham Lincoln.

"BUTTERFLY LADY"
 3½", **$6.00 – 8.00.**
 4¾" juice, **$6.00 – 8.00.**

CHARLES DICKENS CHARACTERS – Gay Fad Studios
Designs, Cottage Cheese, Fagin, 5⅜"; Fat Boy; Mr. Micawber;
Mr. Pickwick; Scrooge; Tiny Tim; **$5.00 – 6.00 each.**
Also made as 9 oz. old-fashioned, **$8.00 – 10 .00.**

CHARLES DICKENS CHARACTER DAVID COPPERFIELD
 Gay Fad Studios Designs, 5⅜", 10½ oz. net weight, Belle
 Vernon Milk Co., Sealtest whipped cream, cottage
 cheese. **$12.00 – 15.00 with red lid.**

TUMBLERS – PRODUCT PACKAGING
PEOPLE & CHARACTERS

CHARACTER SIDE

SONG SIDE

SCOTTSMEN, OLD TIME SONGS SERIES – Big Top Peanut Butter, c. 1950s; also a States Series with Song Sheets on back in this rounded sham (heavy) bottom tumbler. Unmarked. Colors – black, blue, green, orange, red... Over a dozen different characters/songs. Auld Lang Syne, **$8.00 – 10.00**; Comin' Thro' the Rye, **$8.00 – 10.00**.

"PARASOL LADY"
Juice, **$6.00 – 8.00**.

FLORIDA MAP TUMBLER
Big Top peanut butter, **$8.00 – 10.00**.

WATERING CAN LADY/"MISTRESS MARY"
Peanut butter glass, with optic, 4¹⁄₁₆"h,
$14.00 – 18.00.
Also comes in 4½" plain (no optic) red dress version but with bluebirds flying as rim decoration. **$14.00 – 18.00**.

ALSO SEE THE KIDDIE WARE SECTION BEGINNING ON PAGE 84 FOR MORE PRODUCT TUMBLERS WHICH WERE GEARED SPECIFICALLY TOWARDS CHILDREN.

TUMBLERS – SOUVENIR/PLACES

BILLY THE KID MUSEUM –
Ft. Sumner, New Mexico,
4¹¹⁄₁₆", **$12.00 – 15.00.**

WASHINGTON, PENNA. –
"Buy in Glass Festival," 1886 -
1959, Hazel-Atlas No. 1; Hazel-
Atlas No. 2; Typart Valley;
Metro, **$15.00 – 20.00.**

OHIO CAVERNS
W. Liberty, Ohio.
$5.00 – 7.00.

LAND OF LINCOLN
N. Salem State Park, 4⅝".
NIAGARA FALLS
Canada, 5⅛".
NEW MEXICO
White Sands National Monument, 4⅝".
SKYLINE CAVERNS
Front Royal, Virginia, 4⅝".
$5.00 – 7.00 each.

5" SOUVENIR TUMBLERS
Plymouth, Mass., **$5.00 – 7.00.**
Williamsburg, VA, **$5.00 – 7.00.**
Edaville Railroad, South Carver, Mass., **$8.00 – 10.00.**
Sesquicentennial Buckeye State, **$8.00 – 10.00.**
Buffalo Ranch, Oklahoma, **$5.00 – 7.00.**
Weeki Wachi, FL, **$5.00 – 7.00.**

WASHINGTON, D.C., $5.00 – 7.00.
PIKE'S PEAK, $5.00 – 7.00.
MAMMOTH CAVE, KY, $5.00 – 7.00.
LOOKOUT MOUNTAIN, TN, $12.00 – 15.00.
YELLOWSTONE NATIONAL PARK, $5.00 – 7.00.

TUMBLERS – STATES

Evidenced by the number of books being produced on the subject, collecting tumblers of various types is an ever-growing sector of the collectibles field, and the collecting of these souvenir states tumblers of the 1950s is no exception. In fact, we caught a TV program on this subject recently that pronounced these particular souvenir state tumblers an "up and coming collectible," with some states' glasses being worth more than others, depending on their scarcity and/or the demand of a larger volume of people hailing from the larger states. These shown are all of Hazel-Atlas manufacture; but similar versions were produced by Federal Glass. We tried to find representative versions of most states and in that process came across different colors of the same designs, as well as differing state designs. In our experience over the past two years of rather intense searching for Hazel-Atlas items, we found the Platonite ones harder to find than their colorful, frosted cousins.

As for measurements, we're sure they were intended to be 5" tumblers; however, we've found them to be a ⅛" to a ½₂" shy of that measurement in some instances. There was a standard Platonite 5", 12 oz. tapered shell, bead edge tumbler (Cat. #0-364) in their line from the 1920s which appears to have been used throughout their history. We believe that to have been the one used for these states' souvenir line; however, our measurement could only pull a brimming 11 ounces from that tumbler. It appears that a 5", 10 oz., tapered shell, bead edge (possibly their Cat. #1868) was used for the frosted state tumblers which we measured. The differences in the tumblers could be explained by the degree of wear and tear on the mold. So, we're not concerned about the minute differences, but we felt we should point them out. We learned that Illinois has an apple on its state glass. Perhaps you will learn facts you weren't familiar with as you view these. These might be nice teaching tools for children to collect. These were advertised as "map" tumblers in 1952.

ALL STATE TUMBLERS ARE VALUED AT **$6.00 – 8.00** EACH, AND THERE ARE SEVERAL STYLES AVAILABLE. PLATONITE VALUED AT **$8.00 – 10.00**. IF GLASS IS FOUND IN YOUR STATE, EXPECT TO PAY 50% MORE. WESTERN STATES ARE HARDER TO FIND, AND YOU MAY HAVE TO PAY A PREMIUM FOR THEM. WE HAVE FOUND TWO WITH ORIGINAL PRICE STICKERS OF 29 AND 49 CENTS.

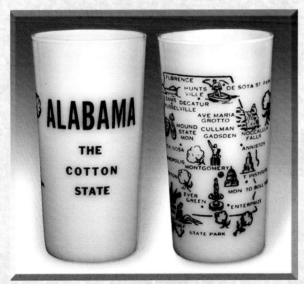

"ALABAMA"
The Cotton State

"ARIZONA"

"ARKANSAS"

TUMBLERS – STATES

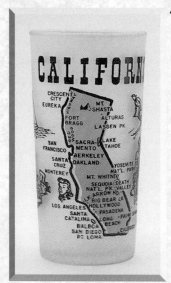

"CALIFORNIA"

"COLORADO"

"FLORIDA"

"GEORGIA"
The Peach State

TUMBLERS – STATES

"ILLINOIS"

"INDIANA"

"IOWA"

"KANSAS"

"KENTUCKY"
The Bluegrass State

"MARYLAND"

"MASSACHUSETTS"
The Bay State

TUMBLERS – STATES

"MICHIGAN"

"MISSOURI"
The Ozark State

"NEBRASKA"

"MONTANA"
The Treasure State

"NEVADA"
The Silver State

"NEW YORK"

"NEW HAMPSHIRE"
Gay Fad Studios Designs
Vertical Ribs
48 States available.

TUMBLERS – STATES

"NORTH CAROLINA"

"OHIO"

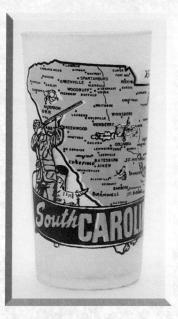

"OKLAHOMA"
The Sooner State

"PENNSYLVANIA"

"SOUTH CAROLINA"

"RHODE ISLAND"

TUMBLERS – STATES

"TENNESSEE"
The Volunteer State

"VIRGINIA"
The Old Dominion

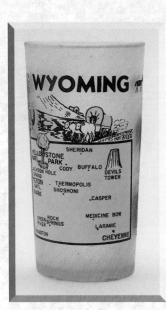

"WYOMING"

"WEST VIRGINIA"

BOTTLES

BABY

OVAL NURSER
7", 8 oz., Cat. #410, dog with doghouse embossing, narrow neck, $20.00 – 25.00.

ROUND NURSER
5⅝", 8 oz., Cat. #970, elephant embossing, marked HA5, $20.00 – 25.00.

ROUND NURSER – 5⅝", 8 oz., Cat. #970, plain, $5.00 – 7.00.

FOOD

NOTICE THE SHAPE AS THIS ALSO CAME AS A 16 OZ. WINE & 32 OZ. DECANTER IN CRYSTAL, RITZ BLUE, AND GREEN.

OLIVE OIL
6¹¹⁄₁₆", slanted, small neck, $8.00 – 10.00.

OIL & VINEGAR
Bottle, 8⅞", 9 oz., Cat. #4549, $5.00 – 7.00 each.
Stopper, Cat. #1881, $2.00 – 3.00.

IT WASN'T UNTIL AFTER THE OWEN'S MACHINES' LEASES WERE NO LONGER VALID THAT HAZEL-ATLAS WAS ENTIRELY FREE TO PRODUCE NARROW, SLOPED-NECK OLIVE BOTTLES EN MASSE FOR THAT TRADE. BEFORE THAT THEY WERE LIMITED TO WIDER MOUTH JARS ON THE AUTOMATED MACHINES BY THEIR CONTRACT WITH OWENS. THE OWENS LINES AT HAZEL-ATLAS WERE SQUARE-SHOULDERED WARES.

WATER

SIX RIB REFRIGERATOR
Crystal, 8⅜"h with lid, Cat. #7571,
32 oz., 1 qt., $8.00 – 10.00.

Not shown:
Seven rib, 64 oz., 2 qt. version,
Cat. #7572, with a centered cap, $15.00 –18.00.

RITZ BLUE
10", 64 oz., oval rib sides, $65.00 – 75.00.
32 oz., $65.00 – 75.00.

INK

CARTER'S WHITE INK
Platonite, 2⅝", 1½ oz., marked HAG16152, $10.00 – 12.00.

SHEFFIELD PRODUCT
Although they also produced inks, doubtless in this type bottle, this one carries oil-based paint of either aluminum or gold used to write in black paged photo albums of the era. $8.00 – 10.00.

CARTER'S WASHABLE BLUE INK
Square shoulder, $12.00 – 15.00.

MEDICINE

EMBOSSED
Milk of Magnesia, The Chas. H. Phillips Chemical Co., Glenbrook, Conn., HA, Made in USA. (not all such bottles were made by Hazel-Atlas; many carry other manufacturers' marks), $10.00 – 15.00.

RIBBED
Ritz Blue, thought to be pharmacy bottle for cough syrups or mixed liquid meds, $12.00 – 15.00.

TALL
Marked HA, $12.00 – 15.00.
SHORT
Marked HA, $10.00 – 12.00.

REFRIGERATOR CLEANER/POISON

PHILCO REFRIGERATOR CLEANER AND POLISH
$15.00 – 20.00.

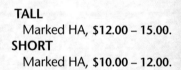

TRIANGULAR – Ritz Blue, embossed hatching, designed so people could tell at once, by touch, that this contained poison. Marked U.C. Co. with HA underneath. $20.00 – 25.00.

POLISHES & OILS

Although Hazel-Atlas had a booming business early on with shoe polish, we could only find one late Shu Mak-Up bottle as an example. Obviously when the polish bottle emptied, it met the trash pile. We did find a few such bottles, but they all carried some other manufacturer's mark. More dirt roads and less money for new shoes were cited in one reference as reasons for the massive market in shoe polishes, of which every family had at least one bottle tucked away. At one time, they came with their own wadding applicator attached to the top so your hands didn't have to touch the messy liquid.

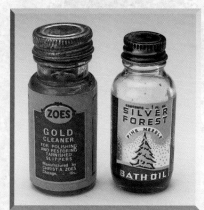

ZOES GOLD TARNISH REMOVER
   3¼"h, 1 oz., marked HA, **$8.00 – 10.00.**

SILVER FOREST BATH OIL
   Pine Needle, 1 oz., marked HA, **$10.00 – 12.00.**

SHU MAK-UP – $3.00 – 5.00.

UNIDENTIFIED PRODUCT BOTTLES

BOTTLE
   Square necked, white cap,
   Cobalt, 4", **$8.00 – 10.00.**

UNIDENTIFIED PRODUCT
   Marked, interesting neck lines,
   $5.00 – 6.00.

Although one of Hazel's earliest products was said to be oil cans to fill the oil lamps of the 1870s, locating examples of their candleholders was not that easily done. Below are some specific pattern examples from the 1930s when every buffet sported a console set of two candles surrounding a large centerpiece bowl, as well as a Star candle (Cat. #930) from which users evidently got years of mileage. That was true of many of Hazel-Atlas's tableware molds! Cathy remembers her grandmother owning one of the small center Star candles. When larger candles got to be the rage, Hazel-Atlas fitted their standby star design with a larger center. If it came as an ashtray, it might also be found in the catalogs as a candle of like design. Both versions of the Star candle also came with indents at the star points to do double duty as a candle and ashes holder.

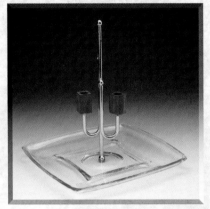

SIMPLICITY COLONY SQUARE MOLD
9¾"h x 9" square, with metal, $12.00 – 15.00.

FLORENTINE NO. 2
Yellow, $30.00 – 35.00.

Not shown:
Crystal, $15.00 – 20.00.
Green, $25.00 – 30.00.

ROYAL LACE – Ruffled edge,
Green, $90.00 – 100.00.

Not Shown:
Crystal, $22.00 – 25.00.
Pink, $70.00 – 80.00.
Ritz Blue, $285.00 – 310.00.

Also available, Straight edge.
Crystal, $18.00 – 20.00.
Green, $45.00 – 50.00.
Pink, $35.00 – 40.00.
Ritz Blue, $80.00 – 85.00.

ROYAL LACE
Rolled edge, to match a like console bowl,
Ritz Blue, $275.00 – 300.00.

Not Shown:
Amethyst (rare), $450.00 – 500.00.
Crystal, $28.00 – 30.00.
Green, $85.00 – 90.00.
Pink, $75.00 – 80.00.

STAR
Small well, Cat. #930,
1⁵⁄₁₆" x 4¹⁹⁄₃₂".
Crystal, $4.00 – 5.00.
Amethyst, $35.00 – 40.00.

STAR
Large well, Cat. #929, 1⅜"h x 4⅞"w, Crystal, $4.00 – 5.00.

CASTERS

Early 1930s furniture often came with rollers on dresser, couch, or bed legs — which would both roll easily and "dent" wood floors or wear holes in linoleum. Casters beneath the legs were the answer to this problem. They came in various colors and sold by the billions. Today, as I sold a couple to a lady, she said they made perfect feeding bowls for her cats.

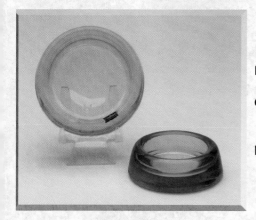

FROST
3", **$5.00 – 7.00.**
GREEN
Cat. #2546, 2⅜", **$6.00 – 8.00.**

Not shown:
Black, 2⅜", **$9.00 – 11.00.**

AMBER – 3", **$8.00 – 10.00.**

COASTERS

"DAISY"
Center with ridges,
3⅜", Cat. #703, **$2.00 – 3.00.**

We were startled to find this similar (marked) Federal Glass Co. example among our thought to be Hazel-Atlas coasters we'd purchased for this book.

ORCHARDWARE – Apple, bridge type coaster, spade & club, **$4.00 – 6.00 each.**

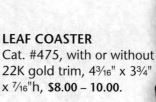

LEAF COASTER
Cat. #475, with or without
22K gold trim, 4³⁄₁₆" x 3¾"
x ⁷⁄₁₆"h, **$8.00 – 10.00.**

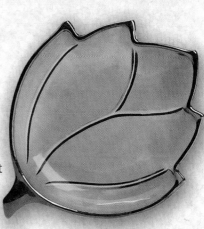

SUNBURST/28 RAYS – 3¾".
Ritz Blue, **$8.00 – 10.00.**

Not shown:
Crystal, **$2.00 – 3.00.**
Green, **$4.00 – 5.00.**
Pink, **$4.00 – 5.00.**

RAYED CENTER – 4¼".
Crystal, **$5.00 – 7.00.**
Ritz Blue, **$10.00 –12.00.**
Note: Rays do not go to center point.

SEE MOROCCAN AMETHYST SWIRL ON PAGE 187 FOR THE OPAL COASTER WHICH WAS SOLD WITH THOSE TUMBLERS.

CONTAINERS

FRUIT/CANNING JARS

There is a whole cadre of fruit jar collectors who know realms more than I about this subject. So go to a book by one of those experts if you want more in-depth knowledge. The first jars were blown, both bottom and neck, separately, and then joined; they showed up in 1858. Producing them was a slow procedure; but suddenly a housewife could cook her summer fruits (hence fruit jars), put them in a jar with a cork seal, and keep them over winter, making winter fare something beyond salted or pickled! For about the next 50 years, the industry struggled to produce caps to seal and preserve the contents within these jars. It wasn't until the early 1900s that housewives could truly seal vegetables from spoilage and cook in the jars themselves — the birth of the canning industry.

These are the products the likes of which helped propel the Hazel-Atlas Company into the realm of the "Big Three" jar manufacturing firms of the twentieth century. By the 1930s there were pretty much Hazel-Atlas, Ball, and Owens-Illinois. They survived the 1929 economic crash by being big enough and automated enough to produce wares more quickly and cheaply and thus to hang on through the crisis. Plus their several factories were well-positioned to carry on business throughout the country. Smaller, hand operated glass companies dropped by the wayside like flies during this financial downturn.

Shown in this section is a zinc type lid for which Hazel-Atlas started producing the Opal liners so the lids wouldn't corrode from the product acids within. However, I believe the original zinc lids may have sealed with a rubber gasket on the shoulder of the jars rather than on the jar rim itself, as this one appears to do. There is a sloped and square shouldered version of the type jars made and various seals of the type used early on in their production. It is my understanding that from around 1909 (Owen's Machine) manufacture, the jars were square shouldered because that was what that machine made and/or that was what Hazel - Atlas was contractually allowed to make.

ATLAS STRONG SHOULDER MASON – 9½"h, marked HA 5082.
The closure on top says:
"The Preston Jar & Closure, pre approved by Good Housekeeping Institute, Serial #2285 Good Housekeeping Mfg."
We presume the jar is elsewhere, but the closure was interesting.
    Liners, crystal, **$4.00 – 5.00 each.**
    Large jar, **$15.00 – 17.00.**
    Small jar, **$3.00 – 5.00.**

$5.00 – 8.00.

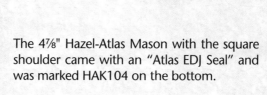

The 4⅞" Hazel-Atlas Mason with the square shoulder came with an "Atlas EDJ Seal" and was marked HAK104 on the bottom.

$5.00 – 8.00.

We have no clue about the amber Atlas Mason with the HA symbol. We rather think this may be some commemorative piece (and/or pure reproduction) rather than an old jar, because Hazel-Atlas was proud of the fact they made mostly flint (crystal) jars and some green ones at the Atlas plant. There was mention of amber snuff bottles, but not amber canning jars in records I read. **$8.00 – 10.00.**

Box, $10.00.

CANISTER JARS

Containers come with various ribbed or paneled patterns. For purposes of identification we have named the three-pillar corner ones that flare at the top into perfect wave lines, "Wave"; the ones that arrow up from a tiny rib at the bottom into graduated ribs of longer lengths to the top, "Graduated Ribs"; and the tall square ones with four ribs in a column at the edge of the jar, "Four Ribbed Column."

DUTCH DECAL CANISTERS – 2 qt., "Wave" corners, **$22.00 – 25.00** each.

DUTCH CANISTER JAR – Marked H3262HA. **$30.00 – 35.00.** At first glance, this appears to be the same 5-3-5 ribbed version as the Old Judge Coffee Jar shown later; however this canister has a square center; the Old Judge has a diamond.

COOK HARD CANDIES – 6¾" "Wave," marked 5217/9, **$20.00 – 22.00.**

CRYSTAL – 8½", marked 5748/8, **$20.00 – 22.00.**

FLASHED PINK – "Wave" corner, rim foot, held Golden Dawn coffee product, **$30.00 – 35.00.**

FLASHED BLUE
"Wave" with flowers, Rim foot, **$30.00 – 35.00.**

FLASHED GREEN WITH BLACK LETTERING – Flour, **$80.00 – 90.00**; sugar, **$80.00 – 90.00**; coffee, **$70.00 – 80.00**; tea, **$60.00 – 70.00.**

FLEUR DE LIS – Diamond pattern, Cross Hatched canisters. Tea, 4⅝", marked: (5188 over 14), **$18.00 – 20.00**; flour, 7¼" (5192 over 10), **$35.00 – 38.00**; coffee, 7¼" (5192 over 15), **$35.00 – 38.00**; sugar, 7¼" (5192 - 6), **$35.00 – 38.00**; salt, 4⅝", (5188 over 14), **$18.00 – 20.00**; spices, showing "Block" design, **$15.00 – 16.00 each.** Note: Owens-Illinois produced a similar jar, but with squares.

PANELED GREEN
$60.00 – 70.00.

FOUR RIBBED COLUMN CANISTERS – Please note that these type jars were also made by Owens-Illinois and that the Hazel-Atlas one shown here had a rose design on the lid. The actual product once sold in these is not identified at this time. **$15.00 – 20.00 each.**

"LANTERN"
Metal trim, 11¼" jar with three-pillar "Wave" corners, ribs at corners flare into wave lines at top, **$22.00 – 25.00.**

"LANTERN"
Metal trim, 9" jar with "Graduated Ribs," small rib at bottom to much longer rib at top, **$18.00 – 20.00.**

ROMAN KEY CANISTER
Marked HA59032, **$35.00 – 40.00.**

CANISTER JARS

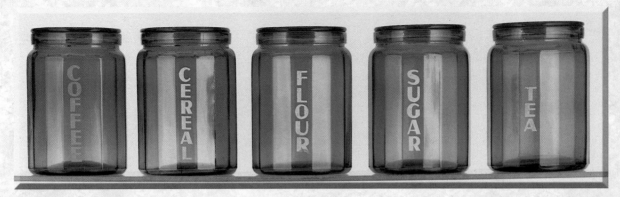

PANELED RITZ BLUE WITH WHITE LETTERING – Coffee, cereal, flour, sugar, and tea $450.00 – 500.00 each.

PRODUCT/PACKING JARS

BLUE BOW SWEET PICKLES
7¼", 1 qt., marked HA 55707, Glaser
Grendell Co., Chic., $12.00 – 15.00.

**CHEZ FRANCOIS CITRUS
FRUIT MARMALADE** – $6.00 – 7.00.

BURMA–SHAVE
4 1/16", 1 lb., $18.00 – 20.00.
2¾", 7 oz., Burma Vita Co., Minneapolis, Minnesota, $15.00 – 16.00.

> **THESE SAYINGS ADVERTISING THIS PRODUCT USED TO BE MOUNTED ON FENCE POSTS ALONG THE HIGHWAY SO THEY COULD BE EASILY READ AS DRIVERS PASSED THEM.**

> **A PEACH LOOKS GOOD WITH LOTS OF FUZZ BUT A MAN'S NO PEACH AND NEVER WUZ.**

> **STATISTICS PROVE NEAR AND FAR THAT FOLKS WHO DRIVE LIKE CRAZY – ARE.**

> **AROUND THE CURVE LICKETY-SPLIT IT'S A BEAUTIFUL CAR WASN'T IT.**

PRODUCT/PACKING JARS

CORONET CHOCOLATES
3¼", 5 oz. (HA 5028), Miami Beach, FL, **$5.00 – 6.00.**

CO-OP GLO-CANDY GLITTER
3½", National Co-operative, Inc., Chic. IL, **$7.00 – 8.00.**

LIBERTY CHERRIES WITH LADY LIBERTY LID
3½", 5 oz., *"Proclaiming liberty throughout the land and to all the inhabitants thereof"* on top of bell, **$12.00 – 15.00.**

SWANKY SWIGS, 1930s – EARLY 1940s

"Why, I remember those. We used them when I was growing up!" or "Look, Mommy, those are like I used at Granny's house!" These are the type comments I often hear when Swanky Swigs are spotted. Serious collectors seek all types and sizes; casual collectors like flowers, particularly daffodils, red tulips, violets, and bachelor buttons. See *Collectible Glassware from the 40s, 50s, 60s...* for later made Swanky Swigs and their metal lids, which have become collectible themselves. Check your local grocery as Kraft has issued two new ones in the spring of 2003. One has stars and stripes; the other one hearts and stripes. A majority, but not all of these have been absolutely documented as Hazel-Atlas production.

For pricing information please refer to *Collector's EncyColpedia of Depression Glass, Sixteenth Edition.*

CANOVA COFFEE
"H" rib jar, $25.00 – 27.00.

MILLAR'S NUT-BROWN COFFEE
Chicago, $18.00 – 20.00.

OLD JUDGE IRRADIATED COFFEE
Settles the Question, $25.00 – 30.00.

MAXWELL HOUSE COFFEE AND CRISCO (CRISCO LID)
6⅛", pebbled rim and bottom (5143 13-3). We also saw an Owens-Illinois version which had the word "Crisco" embossed on the pebbled upper rim of the jar. $15.00 – 18.00.

Maxwell House Coffee Advertisement.

PRODUCT/PACKING JARS
E-Z FREEZE AND STORE JARS

We know a plain jar 16 oz. version of these was in the Hazel-Atlas catalog called an E-Z Freeze Jar, and was provided with a ½" rim head space and a red lid; one even had a ready-made label in the design with "product: date packed." The 18 oz. containers were labeled E-Z Store Jars and purportedly were used by a cottage cheese making concern to market their product. The Pennsylvania Dutch red and black version with the long-tailed bird says, *"A woman's work is never done."* Other designs we located include: **ANTIQUE COAL BUCKET, IVY, MEXICAN SCENE, PAGODA (SMALL,) PAGODA (LARGE,) AND PENNSYLVANIA DUTCH,** $8.00 each $10.00 without lid, $12.00 – 15.00 with lid.

HEINZ JAR
4⁵⁄₁₆", marked HA H-312F4D, Cap marked 33 cents and "refrigerate to retain flavor," $8.00 – 10.00.

HONEYCOMB OR GRAPE CLUSTER EMBOSSED JAR
2"h x 3⅝"w, marked HA25. Lid embossed HA ATLAS, $5.00 – 6.00.

HOWLANDS CURRY POWDER
Geo. Howland Co., Cincinnati, Ohio, 3¾", 1⅛ oz., (shows two lines, punty ball repeated side design), $8.00 – 10.00.

JACK FROST
With shaker lid, 4½", decorator sprinkles, $8.00 – 10.00.

HONEY JAR WITH BAIL
5¼", marked 5623 11, $12.00 – 15.00.

PRODUCT/PACKING JARS
E-Z FREEZE AND STORE JARS

**KRAFT MIRACLE WHIP
SALAD DRESSING**
5⅜", 1 pt., marked HA67462-16, **$10.00 – 12.00.**

KRAFT HANDY PRESERVING JAR
For jams, preserves, pickles, etc., 3¼",
marked HA57624, **$6.00 – 8.00.**

MUSTARD JAR
With spoon, Concentric Ring bottom,
3½", marked HA50475, **$10.00 – 12.00.**

KRAFT
Do Not Freeze, Keep Away from Coils in Refrigerator, marked
HA51752. Cap – *The Great Gildersleeve* comedy show, **$15.00 – 18.00.**

DECO DESIGN PATENTED
Cat. #5455-10,
6"h x 3¼"w, **$10.00 – 12.00.**

PRODUCT/PACKING JARS
PEANUTS/PEANUT BUTTER

SEE GOTHIC PATTERN, PAGE 166 FOR 1950S BIG TOP PEANUT BUTTER PACKING GOBLETS.

JEWEL "T" PEANUT BUTTER
$35.00 – 40.00.

**KROGER'S EMBASSY
PEANUT BUTTER**
$15.00 – 18.00.

EMBOSSED PEANUTS
$35.00 – 40.00.

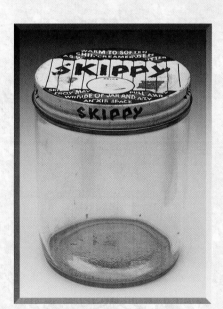

SKIPPY PEANUT BUTTER
$8.00 – 10.00.

PETER PAN CREAMY PEANUT BUTTER
Marked HA2788,
"wave" corner design, **$15.00 – 18.00.**
With intact label, **$20.00 – 22.00.**

SHEDD'S PEANUT BUTTER
Refrigerator jar, with label, $12.00 – 15.00.

PRODUCT/PACKING JARS

PEBBLED BOTTOM
Plain, 4¾" wide mouth, 5⅞"h,
Marked HA 5576, **$6.00 – 8.00.**

"GRADUATED RIBS"
STANLEY E-Z CLEANER
5¼", marked HA501112, 2 lb.
corner design, **$12.00 – 15.00.**

WIRE CLOSURE "LIGHTNING" TYPE
4⅞"h, 1½ pt.; marked HA5-K-643,
$10.00 – 12.00.

WIRE SNAP CLOSURE
4⅞"h; marked HA8 on bottom,
Marked 5374 on side, **$12.00 – 15.00.**

OLD JUDGE TYPE COFFEE JAR
Without label, **$20.00 – 25.00.**

"SQUARES" JAR
5"h; marked HA 10K 8058, Lid - Our Today's Best Buy;
Keep Cool, Do Not Freeze, to ensure freshness keep
closed tightly, **$10.00 – 12.00.**

"DIAMONDS"
7½", marked HA519212, **$15.00 – 18.00.**

PLAIN JAR
With twist-off cap, **$5.00 – 7.00.**

REFRIGERATOR JAR
Storage jar, reusable, marked 5003 F14, lid
marked Veg5003V 2-6. **$5.00 – 6.00.**

COSMETIC & OINTMENT JARS

FACIAL CREAM
With black knobbed screw lid.
Small, 2¾"h x 2¼"w, **$10.00 – 12.00.**
Large, 2½"h x 2¾"w, **$10.00 – 12.00.**

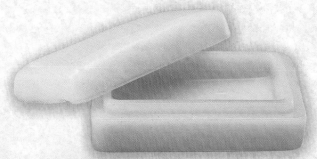

CREAM BOX – Nadinola, a complexion beautifier supposedly used by blacks to lighten their skin. 2" x 3¼", HA marked top, 1885. National Toilet Co., Paris, Tennessee, USA, **$40.00 – 50.00.** Hazel-Atlas referred to these as patch boxes. They were among their first products.

OINTMENT JAR
1⅝"h x 2⅛"w, marked HA, Calendula Cerate, for lacerated wounds, **$10.00 – 12.00.**

SHEPHERD'S OINTMENT
Stearns, KY, 2 oz., 2"h, **$12.00 – 15.00.**

LARGE OINTMENT OR CREAM JAR
4½"h, marked HA14, **$12.00 – 15.00.**

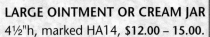

SMALL CRYSTAL JARS
2⅝", marked HAK5482-18, **$6.00 – 8.00 each.**

OINTMENT JAR
2 oz., 2"h; marked HA. Lids – black, painted, or aluminum. Products we've seen in these include: Blue Star, Jim Bourland, Houston, TX mfg., and Heberling's, **$10.00 – 12.00.**

PRESCRIPTION JAR – With label intact, **$6.00 – 8.00.**

COLD CREAM JAR – 2 oz., 2", **$8.00 – 10.00.**

PRINCESS D'AMOUR CLEANSING CREAM
2 oz., 2"h, marked HA, with lid and label, **$12.00 – 15.00.**

POWDER FOUNDATION
3½"h, Society Make-up, Max Factor. Lid – screw type with actor's mask embossed, **$12.00 – 15.00.**

ROSE-PEROXIDE TOILET CREAM
Knapp Extract Co., Cleveland, Ohio, supposedly used by Caucasians to lighten facial hair, 3¹⁵⁄₁₆", marked HA , **$8.00 – 10.00.**

GOLD VEILING, GEORGE BRIARD DESIGN TRIM
With handle & stopper, 5⁹⁄₁₆"h, 5¾ oz.
Cat. #335, $12.00 – 15.00 each.
Colony Square celery, 9½", $8.00 – 10.00.
Roly Poly, 2¼", $4.00 – 5.00.

GOLD/BLACK BAND
With handle & stopper,
5⁹⁄₁₆"h, 5¾ oz., Cat. #335.
$12.00 – 15.00.

SATIN PEACH
Without handle & stopper,
6⅛"h, 5¾ oz., Cat. #4093,
$12.00 – 15.00.
SALT
3⅝", marked HA2-3K
$5.00 – 7.00.

SATIN ROOSTERS – Oil & Vinegar, with
handle & stopper, 5¾ oz., Cat. #335.
$15.00 – 18.00 each.

PINK VEILING
Gay Fad Studios Designs.
$12.00 – 15.00.

SATIN FLORAL
With handle & stopper,
5⁹⁄₁₆"h, 5¾ oz., Cat. #335.
$12.00 – 15.00.

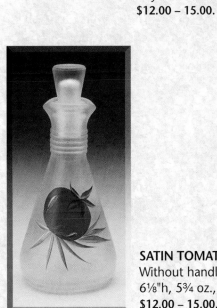

SATIN TOMATO
Without handle, with stopper,
6⅛"h, 5¾ oz., Cat. #4093.
$12.00 – 15.00.

SETS

IVY
Anchor Hocking cruet, 5⅜", **$10.00 – 12.00.**
Shakers, 3⅝", marked HA 2-3, **$5.00 – 7.00 each.**
There is probably a bowl to match.

SATIN ROSE VOGUE
Bowl sham bottom, Cat. #646, **$15.00 – 18.00.**
Cruet – 5¾ oz., marked HA4-8, **$12.00 – 15.00 each.**

SATIN TULIP VOGUE
Bowl (sham bottom), Cat. #646, **$15.00 – 18.00.**
Cruet with handle, Cat. #335, **$12.00 – 15.00 each.**
Shakers 3⅝", marked HA, **$5.00 – 7.00 each.**

Demitasse Sets

You will find these demi-sets plain (Platonite Tableware #0-929) and in myriad decorations or flashed colors for use as after-dinner coffees, or as souvenir products proclaiming where you visited; and some were even made into Kiddie type tea sets with and without accompanying sugar and creamer. (See Moderntone pages 181 – 184). They are 2⁵⁄₃₂"h and come with a 4½" (#0-940) saucer. None that we have seen are marked. A 1946 ad shows them marketed for $7.80 per dozen.

$10.00 – 15.00 EACH — CRYSTAL IS RARE

DECORATED

FLASHED COLORS & SOUVENIR

KIDDIE WARE

Kiddie Items   *by* **HAZEL-ATLAS**

At the risk of offending some older children, we kept the Hazel-Atlas "Kiddie" name for this section of wares. Kiddie bowls appear to mostly come with either red or blue decorations. Six colors may appear in kiddie mugs.

BOWLS

CEREAL BOWLS
5", Cat. #0-268, (Elsewhere #0-626)
Clown-nosed bear, cow, etc., **$12.00 – 15.00.**
Robin Hood, **$25.00 – 30.00.**
Wyatt Earp, **$35.00 – 40.00.**

BOWLS

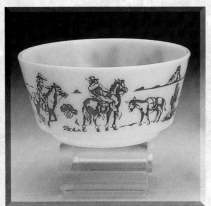

COWBOY AND INDIAN
Cottage cheese bowl, 2⅜"h x 4³¹⁄₃₂"w,
Cat. #0-3422, $15.00 – 18.00.

JOHNNY JUMBO
2⅜"h x 4³¹⁄₃₂"w, Cat. #0-3422,
$18.00 – 20.00.

CISCO KID
Cat. #0-268, $25.00 – 30.00.

GULLIVER'S TRAVELS – All three scenes shown. "SNEAK." "Sneak is the tallest of the spies, And very double jointed, he seems to have a thousand eyes, Whichever way he's pointed." "SNOOP." "Snoop is a chesty sort of guy, Mysterious in makeup, So nimble is this little spy, A leaflet would not shake-up." $25.00 – 30.00.

SCOTTIE DOG
Cereal bowl, refrigerator/cottage
cheese bowl, 2¹³⁄₃₂"h x 4⅞"w,
Cat. #3153, $25.00 – 30.00.

CHILDREN AT PLAY
Cereal, 3"h, flared rim, 5¼"w.
$22.00 – 25.00.

ONE BOWL OF THIS TYPE
WAS SEEN WITH BLUE
AIRPLANES.

"LOONEY TUNES" PIGS
With musical instruments,
Cat. #0-3422, $30.00 – 35.00.

BOWLS

RANGER JOE
Cereal, $20.00 – 25.00.
With wheat as shown, $35.00 – 40.00.

DANCING PIGS
Bowl, 3"h, flared rim, 5¼"w, $20.00 – 22.00.
Sherbet, 3¼", $15.00 – 18.00.
Tumbler, 3⅞", $20.00 – 22.00.

MUGS

ALPHABET – Cat. #0-59 Milk Mug. A serious collector has proposed a theory that there was one alphabet mug for each day of the week and a prayer mug for Sunday.

A, ALLIGATOR – $18.00 – 20.00.
B, BUNNY, $18.00 – 20.00.
D, DONKEY – 2 views, $18.00 – 20.00.

C, COW, 2 views – $18.00 – 20.00.
G, GOOSE, $18.00 – 20.00.
H, HORSE $18.00 – 20.00.

MUGS

MILK MUGS – Cat. #0-59,
  DUCK, BUNNY, DOG – $18.00 – 20.00.
  WYATT EARP – $30.00 – 35.00.
  ROBIN HOOD – $25.00 – 30.00.

MILK MUGS – Cat. #0-59
BUCKING BRONCO – 3"h x 2¹³⁄₁₆"w, $15.00 – 18.00.
HENNY PENNY EGG NOG – $18.00 – 20.00.

SEE PAGE 90 FOR MATCHING BUCKING BRONCO PLATE.

ANIMALS
  Mug, 3⅛"h x 2¹⁵⁄₁₆"w, child, rooster,
  pig, lamb, and duck, $12.00 – 15.00.

Not shown:
  Plate, deep, flat rim, Cat. #0-3211, duck, horse, pig,
  cow, rooster, and lamb, $30.00 – 32.00.
  Plate, divided, flat rim, Cat. #0-3421, $30.00 – 32.00.

FLASHED RED INDIAN
$10.00 – 12.00.

LITTLE RED RIDING HOOD –
3¾", 16 panel bottom, 4-
angle handle, Cat. #0-3404,
$20.00 – 25.00.

CLOWNS – Cat. #0-3404
3¾", 16-panel bottom,
 4-angle handle, $12.00 – 15.00.
 Sherbet, $12.00 – 15.00.

PLATONITE
3¾", 16-panel bottom, 4-angle
handle Cat. #0-3404, $10.00 – 12.00.

Milk Mugs

FLASHED BLUE/FLASHED PINK
3", paneled bottom, 3-angle handle,
$6.00 – 8.00.

SCOTTIE SHERBET – $18.00 – 22.00.

ANIMAL "BAND" MUG
Short, 3", paneled bottom , 3-angle handle, **$22.00 – 25.00.**

BUFFALO BILL
$22.00 – 25.00.

THREE KITTENS WITH LOST MITTENS
Tall, 3¾", 16-panel bottoms, 4-angle handles, Cat. #0-3404, $30.00 – 35.00 each.

PIG WITH FLAG MUG
Short, 3", paneled bottom, 3-angle handle, **$24.00 – 26.00.**

WARRIOR PIG WITH RIFLE
WWII era, tall, 3¾", 16-panel bottom, 4-angle handle,
Cat. #0-3404, **$28.00 – 30.00.**
Tumbler, **$20.00 – 22.00.**

MILK MUGS

FLASHED PINK & TURQUOISE MUGS
Cat. #0-59, $5.00 – 7.00 each.

SPACE MUGS
3⅛"h, indented foot, round handle, $45.00 – 50.00 each.

HOPALONG CASSIDY MILK MUGS
Cat. # 0-59, $30.00 – 35.00 each.
Colors: Red, black, blue, green.

THESE MUGS HAVE BEEN FOUND WITH BIG TOP PEANUT BUTTER LIDS, INDICATING THEY, TOO, WERE PACKAGING CONTAINERS FOR W.T. YOUNG FOOD CORP., THE MANUFACTURER OF THAT BRAND.

PLATES/MUGS

PLATES
7", Cat. #0-3222.
**DOG, CAT, DUCK,
 SQUIRREL, OWL** – $20.00 – 25.00.
ROBIN HOOD – $30.00 – 35.00.
WYATT EARP – $30.00 – 35.00.

ALPHABET DISH
Cat. #0-61, divided with rim sides, 6⅝", $40.00 – 45.00.
CLOWN MILK MUG
Cat. #0-59, easy to find, $10.00 – 12.00.

PLATES/MUGS

DAVY CROCKETT
  Mug, $18.00 – 20.00.
    Flashed color, $20.00 – 22.00.
  Plate, $30.00 – 35.00.
    Flashed color, $35.00 – 40.00.

TEX
  Mugs, six colors, orange not shown.
  $12.00 – 15.00 each.
BUCKING BRONCO
  Plate, $30.00 – 35.00.

SHIRLEY TEMPLE

CEREAL BOWL*
  With hexagons, $50.00 – 60.00.
MUG*
  3¹¹⁄₁₆", 4-angle handle, $50.00 – 55.00.
CREAM PITCHER*
  4³⁄₁₆", 4-angle handle (style most often used), $30.00 – 35.00.

QUAKER PUFFED WHEAT ADVERTISEMENT
  $250.00 – 275.00.

*BEWARE OF REPRODUCTIONS!

SHIRLEY TEMPLE

FRONT

BACK

CREAM PITCHER
Modernistic/"Colonial Block" mold, rare, **$1,000.00 – 1,250.00.**

RELIGIOUS

Here are some examples of the religious sayings which Hazel-Atlas produced on their Kiddie wares.

"WE GIVE THEE THANKS O GOD!"
Cereal bowl, Cat. #0-3422, **$20.00 – 25.00.**

"JESUS LOVES ME"
Divided dish, Cat. #0-61,
6¾", **$40.00 – 45.00.**

**"LORD I THANK THEE FOR TODAY, FOR MY FOOD,
MY WORK, MY PLAY"**
Milk mug, black lettering, Cat. #0-59, **$20.00 – 25.00.**

**"THE FOOD GOD GIVES WILL MAKE ME GROW,
HOW GOOD GOD IS TO LOVE ME SO"**
Cereal bowl, Cat. #0-3422, **$20.00 – 25.00.**

**"JESUS LOVES THE LITTLE CHILDREN, ALL THE
CHILDREN OF THE WORLD"**
Milk mug, black lettering, Cat. #0-59, **$20.00 – 25.00.**

RELIGIOUS

"JESUS LOVES THE LITTLE CHILDREN"
Milk mug, red lettering, Cat. #0-59,
$20.00 – 25.00.

"LOVE ONE ANOTHER"
Plate, 7", Cat. #0-3222.
$30.00 – 35.00.

"BE YE KIND ONE TO ANOTHER"
Milk tumbler, 2⅞"h x 3"top,
Cat.#0-165, flared rim, $20.00 – 25.00.

TUMBLERS

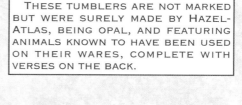

THESE TUMBLERS ARE NOT MARKED BUT WERE SURELY MADE BY HAZEL-ATLAS, BEING OPAL, AND FEATURING ANIMALS KNOWN TO HAVE BEEN USED ON THEIR WARES, COMPLETE WITH VERSES ON THE BACK.

ALPHABET TUMBLERS – 4⅝", with flared rims. We have learned there is an "H" for Horse in this series; there is also a 3" version available.

COW – "C is for Cow, Always gentle and sweet, She gives us the milk, That makes each meal a treat."

DUCK – "D is for Duckling, With eyes big and round, He floats on the water, And swims sitting down."

LAMB – "L is for lamb, With fleece white and curly, He plays hard all day, And then goes to bed early." **$20.00 – 25.00 each.**

CLOWN
Cat. #0-364, **$15.00 – 18.00.**

TUMBLERS

JACK AND JILL – Two views, $22.00 – 25.00.

COW
With various marking lines
for liquid, 5⅛"h x 2⅞"w,
$20.00 – 25.00.

CIRCUS
3⅞", Cat. #0-165, marked HA,
$18.00 – 20.00.

MARY HAD A LITTLE LAMB
$22.00 – 25.00.

OLD KING COLE
3⅞", 8 oz., Cat. #0-358,
$25.00 – 30.00.

RED RIDING HOOD & WOLF
3⅞"h x 2¾"w, unmarked,
$22.00 – 25.00.

PRODUCT PACKAGING

The following tumblers were used to package products, but were geared to children's interests and/or education. Tumbler product packaging was a huge part of Hazel-Atlas's business from the early 1900s onward. A magazine of the 1930s termed it the world's largest tumbler producer. They always made them at their Clarksburg plant.

As you can see from the label still attached to the Queen of Hearts tumbler on page 95, this tumbler held some manufacturer's homogenized peanut butter product. (There is also a story of these containing Wisconsin cheese products, so there were probably other products as well). I have no idea how many different tumblers there are; these are the ones we found. (I remember studying in college that some of these rhymes were thought to be sly barbed witicisms made up about the English court personalities of the day; alas! I do not remember which referred to whom! I think "my black hen" was a reference to Elizabeth I, dressed in mourning black, parceling grants or boons of money (eggs) for this and that cause or expedition). Children love the rhymes, even if the subtle jests toward personages of the realm have been long lost. You will notice there are versions depicting WWII vehicles, which is believed to be the general timeframe for these.

These ribbed or optic glasses measure 4¹⁄₁₆"h and have a rim lip or band.

TUMBLERS
PRODUCT PACKAGING

CINDERELLA – "Cinderella wed the prince, And lived happily ever after." $25.00 – 30.00.

QUEEN OF HEARTS
"The Queen of Hearts, She made some tarts, All on a summer's day, The Knave of Hearts, He stole the tarts, And took them clean away," $20.00 – 25.00.

DOODLE DOODLE DOO
"Doodle Doodle Doo, The Princess lost her shoe, Her highness hopped, The fiddler stopped, Not knowing what to do," $20.00 – 25.00.

HUMPTY DUMPY – "Humpty Dumpty sat on a wall, Humpty Dumpty had a great fall, All the king's horses and all the king's men, Couldn't put Humpty together again,"

A FROG – "A frog he would a-wooing go, Whether his mother would let him or no, With a rowley, powley, gammon & spinich, Hey Ho says Anthony Rowley,"

OLD KING COLE – "Old King Cole was a merry old soul, And a merry old soul was he, He called for his pipe, He called for his bowl, And he called for his fiddler's three,"

$20.00 – 25.00 each.

TUMBLERS
PRODUCT PACKAGING

RED RIDING HOOD – "Red Riding Hood meets the wolf, on the way to grandmother's."

MARY & LAMB – "Mary had a little lamb, Its fleece was white as snow, And every place that Mary went, The lamb was sure to go,"

JOLLY OLD PIG – A jolly old pig once lived in a sty, And three little piggies had she, And she waddled about saying Grumph! Grumph! Grumph! While the little ones said "Wee! Wee!"

OLD MOTHER HUBBARD – "Old mother Hubbard went to her cupboard,"

HICKETY PICKETY – "Hickety Pickety, My black hen, She lays eggs, For gentlemen, Sometimes nine, Sometimes ten, Hickety Pickety, My black hen,"

LITTLE BOY BLUE – "Little boy blue come blow your horn, The sheep are in the meadow, The cows are in the corn, But where's the little boy who looks after the sheep, He's under the haystack, fast asleep,"

JACK & JILL – "Jack and Jill went up the hill to fetch a pail of water; Jack fell down and broke his crown, and Jill came tumbling after,"

OLD WOMAN IN SHOE – "There was an old woman who lived in a shoe; She had so many children she didn't know what to do; She gave them some broth without any bread, She whipped them all soundly, And sent them to bed,"

$20.00 – 25.00 each.

WE HAVE SINCE HEARD ABOUT A SIMPLE SIMON; PUSSY CAT, PUSSY CAT; AND GOOSEY GOOSEY GANDER.

TUMBLERS
PRODUCT PACKAGING

DESTROYER "SELFRIDGE"
Speed exceeds 35 knots, with eight 34 guns
Quarters for 210 men, **$25.00 – 30.00.**

ARMOR SCOUT, JEEP
WWII, 4⅛", same peanut butter type glass,
$25.00 – 30.00.

BILLY BULL, CHIPMUNK,
"One of the Short Stump Gang",
SAMMY SQUIRREL, SYLVESTER SKUNK, WILLIE WORM
Set – 5"h, frosted, marked HA, **$8.00 – 10.00 each.**

EDUCATIONAL

COLT 45 PEACEMAKER
"The sixes that won the west"
series, **$8.00 – 10.00.**

ASTRONAUT
NASA capsule,
Marked HA.
$10.00 – 12.00.

ADMIRAL DEWEY
Naval hero of Manila, 5¼",
marked HA, **$8.00 – 10.00.**

DAVY CROCKETT
Coonskin Congressman, Indian
Fighter, Hero of the Alamo,
Frontier Hero, 1786 – 1836,
$12.00 – 15.00.

TUMBLERS
FANTASY

FANTASY GLASS
Series of five, marked HA, held a tea product;

WARRIORS
With helmets, ax, & blade, green,

PIRATES, yellow

COWBOYS, orange

SPACE WALKER, blue

INDIANS, pink; $10.00 – 12.00 each.

KITCHENWARE

BATTER JUGS & SYRUPS

The 9¼" tall, concentric ring batter jugs shown are marked "HA55789." We believe the frosted pitcher shown with the tulip designed waffle/syrup to be Federal's #175 plain jug.

Since this set was decorated elsewhere (possibly by Gay Fad), it was a common occurrence for decorator firms to mix wares from the several companies from whom they bought plain wares. The floral decorated syrup is not marked but has a daisy type embossed design where the HA logo was generally placed. We believe these to be Hazel-Atlas wares made for some company who did not want the glassware company mark there.

Please note the label on the no-drip server touts its 32- ounce use for cocktails as well as batters, milk, hot chocolate or chilling ice water.

The indented paneled bottom syrups, 9"h with lid (marked HA 5054) and 5⅜"h with lid (marked HA 5049) are both marked "Federal Tool Company, Chicago." I presume they made the closures.

At a show recently we encountered a concentric ring bottom batter jug (marked HA) with a red, slick handle pouring spout which touted it as being a "Dripless Pitcher by Androck."

You will see a similar type handle on the "HA 110 24" Tulip syrup. The Androck red handle went straight across whereas that slick syrup handle of the Federal Tool Company slopes a bit upward.

The concentric ring syrups and the tulip optic one all have the daisy mark in the center ring in the bottom. The overlapping leaves design with the graceful slick handle curvature says Federal Tool Corp., Chicago, and is marked "HA 110 - 24." The shakers shown with the slick handle syrup are the same overlapping leaf design and are marked "HA 5108" (orange cone top), and "HA 5048" (flat red top).

ROSEMALING DESIGN WAFFLE SET
Gay Fad Studios
Batter dispenser, 48 oz., $35.00 - 40.00.
Syrup, 11½ oz., $30.00 - 35.00.
Federal pitcher, 85 oz., $30.00 - 35.00.

Not shown:
Beverage tumbler, 12 oz., $8.00 - 10.00.
Juice tumbler, 4 oz., $5.00 - 7.00.
Square Federal "Star" juice pitcher, $25.00 - 30.00.

BATTER JUGS & SYRUPS

POPPY DESIGN
Gay Fad Studios, c.1952.
Batter jug, 9¼"h, with lid,
marked HA 5378 9, 48 oz., **$35.00 – 40.00.**
Syrup/cream (in 4 pc. utility set)/ touch sugar,
5½"h, daisy mark on bottom, **$25.00 – 30.00.**

Not shown:
Beverage pitcher, **$30.00 - 35.00.**
Tumbler, 12 oz., **$8.00 - 10.00.**
Juice pitcher, **$25.00 - 30.00.**
Tumbler, 4 oz., **$5.00 - 7.00.**
Gravy mixer, **$25.00 - 30.00.**
Nut chopper, **$25.00 - 30.00.**

BATTER JUG
9"h, with lid, marked HA 5054,
Federal Tool Corp., Chic., **$18.00 – 22.00.**

SYRUP
5⅜"h, with lid marked HA 5049,
Federal Tool Corp., Chic., **$12.00 – 15.00.**

"SAMBO"
Gay Fad Studios Designs
Batter, **$115.00 – 125.00.**
Syrup, **$115.00 – 125.00.**
Set on white plastic tray, **$275.00.**

DAISY MARK SYRUP
7¾", with lid, **$15.00 – 18.00.**

OVERLAPPING LEAVES DESIGN
Syrup, Federal Tool Corp., Chicago,
marked HA 110 24, **$12.00 – 15.00.**
Shakers marked HA 5108 6 and HA 5108K4,
$4.00 – 5.00 each.

BATTER JUGS & SYRUPS

YELLOW HANDLE SYRUP
$8.00 – 10.00.

RED SYRUP – $18.00 – 20.00.

BLUE SYRUP – $18.00 – 20.00.

NO DRIP SERVERS
Federal Tool Corp.,
1 qt., $12.00 – 15.00.
1 pt., $15.00 – 18.00.

ADVERTISED FOR USE AS BEVERAGE OR DRINK
SERVERS AS WELL AS WAFFLE/SYRUP SETS.

BOWLS

These same type bowls were shown in the Kiddie section with scenes appropriate for children. They were also made for adult use as cereals, drippings, or utility bowls (when a lid was added, shown on page 118), and they were product packing containers for cottage cheese as well.

Cottage Cheese Bowls

by **HAZEL-ATLAS**

RED MAPLE LEAF
Cat. #0-3422, $18.00 – 20.00.
BLUE WILLOW
Cat. #0-3422, $10.00 – 15.00.
STRAWBERRIES
Cat. #0-3422, $10.00 – 15.00.
GREEN IVY
Cat. #0-3422, $10.00 – 15.00.

BOWLS

DAISIES ON BLUE
$10.00 – 12.00.

FRONT

BACK
DRIPPINGS JAR WITH LID
2¾"h x 5"w, $30.00 – 35.00.

Later issues listed under
WHITEWARE cereals –
Avocado, (6007),
Blue (6005),
Gold (6006),
Poppy (6004), Cat. #W567,
2"h x 5"w, **$4.00 – 5.00 each.**

GREEN IVY UTILITY
Cat #0-3422, 5" round, **$22.00 – 25.00.**

FLASHED BLUE
Has been found with large metal
cover with HA embossed in lid.
2¾"h x 5"w, flared rim.
$8.00 – 10.00.

PATRIOTIC ADVERTISING STARS BOWL – Cereal/cottage cheese, 2¾"h x 5"w, **$30.00 – 35.00.**

BOWLS

CHECKERBOARD – 2⅛"h x 4⅞"w, blue, green, and yellow mugs bowls (loop handles), $6.00 – 8.00 each

"DOTS" – 2"h, x 4⅞"w, blue, poppy, $6.00 – 8.00 each.

CRISS CROSS – A PATTERN OF KITCHENWARE

This ware has long caught the eyes of collectors, and judging from the myriad treatments and/or colors of the glassware products, it must have been a very good selling line for the company. We know from a 1938 catalog that it was in production in colors of crystal, green, and pink. The Platonite bowls were purportedly cottage cheese product containers from the 1950s. Do notice that these type bowls have a kind of pyramid protrusion where the lines cross each other, rather than the square, as in other pieces. Really hard to find pieces include the sugar with lid, creamer, 54 oz. water pitcher with ice lip, the 9 oz. water tumbler, 64 oz. water jar, and the 5½" round refrigerator jar. The pitcher and tumbler were only produced in crystal.

COTTAGE CHEESE BOWLS
Various flashed colors, 3¼"h x 5"w, $12.00 – 15.00 each.

FOOD MIXER
With handle, baby face on side, $85.00 – 90.00.

PACKERS JAR
$75.00 – 85.00.

BUTTER DISH
¼ lb., fired green, $60.00 – 65.00.

CRISS CROSS

CRYSTAL AND PINK

Row 1: 9⅝" mixing bowl, **$40.00 – 45.00**; 8¾" mixing bowl, **$35.00 – 40.00**; 7⅝" mixing bowl, **$30.00 – 35.00**.

Row 2: 6⅝" mixing bowl, **$25.00 – 30.00**; 4" x 4" refrigerator bowl, with cover, **$30.00 – 35.00**; creamer, **$60.00 – 65.00**; butter, 1 lb., **$60.00 – 65.00**.

Row 3: Orange reamer, **$300.00 – 335.00**; lemon reamer, **$40.00 – 45.00**; butter, ¼ lb., **$65.00 – 70.00**; round 5½" refrigerator bowl with cover, **$295.00 – 325.00**.

Row 4: Creamer, **$25.00 – 30.00**; sugar, **$20.00 – 25.00**; sugar lid, **$45.00 – 50.00**; Cobalt round 5½" refrigerator bowl with cover **$300.00 – 325.00**; refrigerator dish (like butter), **$295.00 – 335.00**.

Row 5: 64 oz. water bottle, **$40.00 – 45.00**; 32 oz. water bottle, **$35.00 – 40.00**; 54 oz. pitcher, **$150.00 – 175.00**; 4" x 8" refrigerator bowl, with cover, **$20.00 – 25.00**; 8" x 8" refrigerator bowl, with cover, **$25.00 – 30.00**.

CRISS CROSS

RITZ BLUE

Row 1: Butter, 1 lb., **$135.00 – 145.00**; butter, ¼ lb., **$135.00 – 145.00**; orange reamer, **$300.00 – 325.00**.

Row 2: 8" x 8" refrigerator bowl, with cover, **$135.00 – 145.00**; 4" x 8" refrigerator bowl, with cover, **$115.00 – 125.00**; 4" x 4" refrigerator bowl, with cover, **$42.00 – 48.00**.

Row 3: 7⅝" mixing bowl, **$65.00 – 70.00**; 6⅝" mixing bowl, **$50.00 – 55.00**; 3½" x 5¾" refrigerator dish (like butter), **$135.00 – 145.00**;

Row 4: 10⅝" mixing bowl, **$120.00 – 135.00**; 9⅝" mixing bowl, **$85.00 – 95.00**; 8¾'" mixing bowl, **$80.00 – 90.00**. Set of five mixing bowls, **$400.00 – 450.00**.

CRISS CROSS

GREEN

Row 1: 64 oz. water bottle, $165.00 – 175.00; 32 oz. water bottle, $150.00 – 165.00; creamer, $60.00 – 65.00; sugar, $40.00 – 45.00; sugar lid, $85.00 – 100.00.

Row 2: 8" x 8" refrigerator bowl, with cover, $80.00 – 85.00; 4" x 8" refrigerator bowl, with cover, $65.00 – 75.00; 3½" x 5¾" refrigerator dish, butter-like, $75.00 – 80.00; 4" x 4" refrigerator bowl, with cover, $30.00 – 35.00.

Row 3: Butter, 1 lb., $60.00 – 65.00; butter, ¼ lb., $65.00 – 70.00; orange reamer, $35.00 – 40.00.

Row 4: 10⅝" mixing bowl, $55.00 – 60.00; 9⅝" mixing bowl, $40.00 – 45.00; 8¾" mixing bowl, $35.00 – 40.00; 7⅝" mixing bowl, $30.00 – 35.00; set of five mixing bowls, $195.00 – 210.00.

GREENWARE – c. 1929

We know that the first colored tableware (other than the opal they had from their beginning) was green glass made in 1929. Until the October financial crash, 1929 was looking to be a really good year for the firm. They launched a new factory in California, a line of new colored kitchenware and tableware (Modernistic) and their gross production figures were 35,688,000 — resulting in a per capita gain from 1925 of around 41 percent!

Below are examples of some of their first green ware offerings. Others were under refrigerator items, milk pitchers, casters, measuring cups (1 spout), canisters, reamers, range shakers, etc., plus the Modernistic ("Colonial Block") pattern. That pattern appears to have already existed in crystal, but having it in green was new.

BOWLS – Cereal, many optic (also shown in crystal with green trim), green 3¹⁵⁄₁₆", **$4.00 – 5.00**; green 5", **$5.00 – 6.00**; crystal with green, **$3.00 – 4.00**.

BUTTER
Top embossed "Butter Cover," Cat. #G-2013 (& ½), **$60.00 – 65.00**.

BOWLS
Fancy, Cat. #G-732, The first offerings were not crimped around the edges.
  8", straight, **$15.00 – 18.00**.
  4⅝", crimped, **$8.00 – 10.00**.

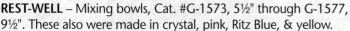

REST-WELL – Mixing bowls, Cat. #G-1573, 5½" through G-1577, 9½". These also were made in crystal, pink, Ritz Blue, & yellow.

5½", **$18.00 – 20.00**.	6½", **$22.50 – 25.00**.
7½", **$25.00 – 27.50**.	8½", **$30.00 – 32.50**.
9½", **$35.00 – 40.00**.	

JELL-O MOLD
Individual, 2"h x 2⅞"w, marked HA (believed to have been a premium item for Jell-O, possibly for use with the new lime flavor offered in 1930), **$6.00 – 8.00**.

Not shown:
  Crystal, **$3.00 – 5.00**.

COLONIAL TUMBLER
  4⅛", 7-panel, Cat. #389, **$6.00 – 8.00**.
ORANGE REAMER
  With seed dam, Cat. #G-72, **$25.00 – 28.00**.
SYRUP
  6⅛"h, 11 oz., Cat. #G-866, **$50.00 – 55.00**.

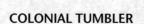

MEASURING CUPS

1 CUP – 3 spout, cobalt blue, $300.00 – 350.00; 3 spout, yellow, $300.00 – 350.00; 3 spout, unembossed pink $35.00 – 40.00; 3 spout, unembossed green, $30.00 – 35.00; 3 spout, embossed "Urban's Liberty Flour,"$75.00 – 85.00.

1 CUP – 3 spout, red flashed, $55.00 – 65.00; 3 spout, green flashed, $55.00 – 65.00; 3 spout, opalescent white, $45.00 – 55.00; 3 spout, flat white, with red trim, $55.00 – 65.00; 3 spout, embossed Kellogg's, pink, $40.00 – 45.00.

1 CUP – 3 spout embossed Kellogg's, green, $35.00 – 40.00; 1 spout, pink, $35.00 – 40.00; 1 spout, green, $30.00 – 35.00.

2 CUPS – Handle at back to show design. White with red/black dots, $55.00 – 60.00; white with blue dots, $55.00 – 60.00; green with white dots, $50.00 – 60.00; Black Floral decal, $55.00 – 60.00.

MEASURING CUPS

2 CUP – White with decorated bands, **$45.00 – 50.00 each**; white, **$25.00 – 30.00**; opalescent white, **$25.00 – 30.00**; Fired-on red, **$55.00 – 60.00**.

2 CUP – Note handle shape. Yellow, **$275.00 – 295.00**; iridized, **$100.00 – 125.00**; green, **$50.00 – 55.00**; cobalt blue, **$250.00 – 275.00**.

4 CUP – Frosted green, **$30.00 – 35.00**.

4 CUP – Green, marked A&J, **$30.00 – 35.00**; white with black trim, **$40.00 – 45.00**.

MECHANICAL ATTACHMENTS

PINK BEATER
$60.00 – 70.00.

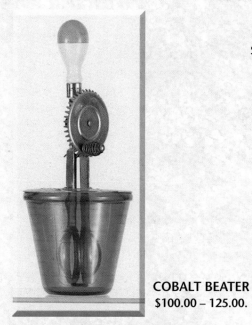

COBALT BEATER
$100.00 – 125.00.

MIXER, BOTTOM ONLY
$6.00 – 8.00.

NUT GRINDER
$8.00 – 10.00.

RENWAL ELECTRIC VAPORIZER
WITH HAZEL-ATLAS JAR
$12.00 – 15.00 with box.

FOOD CHOPPERS
12½"h, 4¾" base, $10.00 – 12.00.
8½"h, 4½" base, $6.00 – 8.00.
7½"h, 4" base, $6.00 – 8.00.
1½ cup, 4⅞" base, $6.00 – 8.00.

MIXING BOWLS

CATTAIL – 4⅞", 64 oz., Cat. #0-524. This style was late 1950s, mirroring the Hocking Splash-proof look of mixing bowls, **$20.00 – 25.00.**

"MODERNTONE" RINGS – This bowl is believed to have been made by Hazel-Atlas. It isn't marked and was part of a set of mixing bowls which came with a mixer of the genre of late 1940s and early 1950s Sunbeam and Hamilton Beach styles. However, we did find a catalog picture of a cottage cheese packing bowl with the same look, though a rim had been added to hold the lid for the packing container.

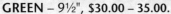

GREEN – 9½", **$30.00 – 35.00.**

OPAL
4¼"h x 4³⁄₁₆"w, **$15.00 – 18.00.**

PILLAR OPTIC RIBBED WITH SQUARED BASE – Believed to have been instituted in the late 1930s or early 1940s. These came in sets of five bowls, sizes of 6⅝" – 11⅝". They were also made in green and pink, which is shown at the top of the next page. You should know that a very similar bowl was made by Bartlett-Collins in the early 1940s which you often see decorated with red stripes; however, these came as a set of three in 6", 8", and 10" sizes. Don't confuse these with the ribbed Hazel-Atlas ones.

AMETHYST
9⅝", **$40.00 – 45.00.**

CRYSTAL
7⅝", **$10.00 – 12.00.**

MIXING BOWLS

PILLAR OPTIC RIB, PINK
9⅝", $30.00 – 35.00.
7⅝", $20.00 – 25.00.

PILLAR OPTIC RIB, RITZ BLUE
10⅝", $85.00 – 95.00.
11⅝", $110.00 – 125.00.

REST-WELL – Cat. #1573 –1577, set of five, sizes 5½" – 9½". Examples of green are shown on page 106.

PINK
9½", $35.00 – 40.00.	8½", $30.00 – 32.50.
7½", $25.00 – 27.50.	6½", $22.50 – 25.00.

Not shown:
5½", $18.00 – 20.00.

YELLOW
9½", $35.00 – 40.00.	8½", $30.00 – 35.00.
7½", $22.00 – 25.00.	6½", $18.00 – 20.00.

Not shown:
5½", $18.00 – 20.00.

RITZ BLUE
Restwell, 5½", $30.00 – 35.00.
Plain, 6", $30.00 – 35.00.

MIXING BOWLS

MIXING BOWLS . . . and SETS

2 Big Features

1. ROLLED EDGE—Prevents chipping and makes an easy grip for handling.
2. PANELED BASE — Permits bowls to be placed in tilted position. Heavy pressed glass.

7 in., pressed, handled and lipped. 1 doz in carton, 23 lbs.

50R-3250—Crystal
Doz **$1.08**

50R-3251—Green
Doz **1.25**

4-Pc. Sets—Green
5, 6, 7 and 8 in. bowls, pressed.
50R-3293—½ doz sets in carton, 44 lbs.
Doz sets **4.50**

5-Pc. Sets—Green
5, 6, 7, 8 and 9 in. bowls, pressed.
50R-3295—1/12 doz sets in carton.
Doz sets **6.25**

Green Individual Sizes
Weights in order listed: 30 lbs, 40 lbs, 50 lbs, 24 lbs, 33 lbs

	In.	Doz in ctn	Doz
50R-3270	5½	3	.78
50R-3271	6½	3	.85
50R-3272	7½	3	1.05
50R-3273	8½	1	1.50
50R-3274	9½	1	1.95

5-Pc. Sets
5½, 6½, 7½, 8½ and 9½ in. bowls. 1/12 doz sets in carton, 9 lbs.
50R-3296—Green
Doz sets **6.95**

PLAINWARE
Line 777, set of five,
Cat. #773-777, sizes 5", 6", 7", 8", 9".
6", $20.00 – 25.00.
5", $18.00 – 20.00.

Not shown:
7", $25.00 – 28.00.
8", $28.00 – 32.00.
9", $32.00 – 35.00.

GREEN IVY
4", $8.00 – 10.00.
6", $10.00 – 12.00.
7", $12.00 – 15.00.
9", $15.00 – 18.00.
Cereal, $10.00 – 12.00.

Not shown:
8", $15.00 – 18.00.

SCALLOPED RIM
Cat. #6265, late set sold in four,
5" – 8", or three, 6"– 8".
8", $20.00 – 22.00.

Not shown:
5", $10.00 – 12.00.
6", $12.00 – 15.00.
7", $15.00 – 18.00.

FLASHED COLORS – 2 sets. Although the catalog gives even figure measurements, the smaller marked bowls in yellow and green measure 5 1/16" and 4⅞", respectively.
5", $10.00 – 12.00; 6", $11.00 – 13.00; 7", $12.00 – 15.00.

MIXING BOWLS

OPAL WITH DOTS – Red or yellow, 5", **$15.00 – 18.00**; 6" (not shown), **$15.00 – 18.00**; 7", **$20.00 – 25.00**; 8", **$25.00 – 30.00**; 9" (not shown), **$30.00 – 35.00**.

PLATONITE
With Red Band between black hairline
MIXING BOWL
5", **$12.00 – 15.00**.
6", **$12.00 – 15.00**.
UTILITY JAR
$22.00 – 25.00.

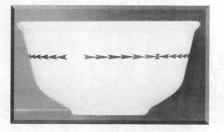

**PLATONITE WITH RED ARROWS
BAND**, 8", **$25.00 – 30.00**.

RED STRAWBERRY – The catalog sheet shows that these Platonite bowls were shipped from Washington, Pennsylvania — not Clarksburg, West Virginia. I mention that for the slight controversy over which plant made what wares. 5", **$8.00 – 10.00**; 6", **$10.00 – 12.00**; 7", **$12.00 – 15.00**; 8", **$15.00 – 18.00**.

ROOSTERS
6" (shown on pg. 35), **$20.00 – 22.00**.
7", **$22.00 – 25.00**.
8", **$25.00 – 30.00**.

MIXING BOWLS

DUTCH COUPLE AND WINDMILL
9" x 4½"h, **$30.00 – 35.00.**
8" x 3⅞"h, **$28.00 – 30.00.**
7" x 3⅜"h, **$22.50 – 25.00.**
6" x 3"h, **$22.00 – 25.00.**
5" x 2½"h, **$15.00 – 20.00.**

"SKATING DUTCH"
Round utility bowl, 5¾", Cat. #0-569, **$30.00 – 35.00.**
Small cottage cheese bowl, 2⅜"h x 5"w, **$14.00 – 15.00.**
Mixing bowls:
5" x 2½"h, **$15.00 – 20.00.**
6" x 3"h, **$22.00 – 28.00.**
7" x 3⅜"h, **$22.00 – 28.00.**
8" x 3⅞"h, **$28.00 – 30.00.**
9" x 4½"h, **$30.00 – 35.00.**

DUTCH CHILDREN
Red, 7", Cat. #0-3422, **$20.00 – 25.00.**

2 CUP PITCHER AND REAMER SETS

Row 1: Yellow, **$350.00 – 375.00**; cobalt blue, **$325.00 – 350.00**; pink, **$155.00 – 165.00**; green, **$65.00 – 70.00**.

Row 2: Criss Cross reamers, cobalt blue, **$275.00 – 300.00**; pink, **$295.00 – 325.00**; crystal, **$20.00 – 25.00**; green, **$35.00 – 40.00**.

Row 3: Green, tab handled, **$28.00 – 30.00**; decorated 2 cup sets, ea. **$55.00 – 65.00**; fired-on red set, **$65.00 – 70.00**.

Row 4: Decorated sets, ea., **$55.00 – 65.00**; tumbler to match, **$12.00 – 15.00**.

Row 5: Criss Cross, tab handled,
Pink, **$325.00 – 355.00**; green, **$40.00 – 45.00**; crystal, **$20.00 – 22.00**; green, **$28.00 – 30.00**.

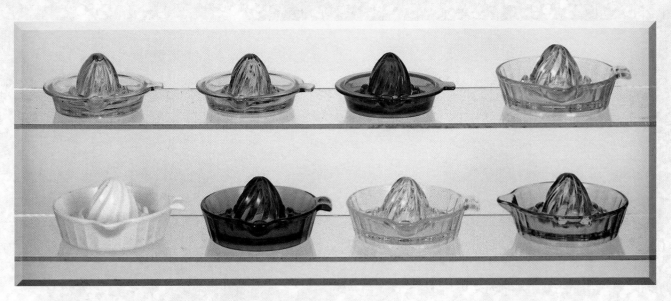

REAMERS

Row #1 Small tab handled reamer, pink, **$45.00 – 48.00**; green lemon reamer, Cat. #6175, **$25.00 – 28.00**; cobalt blue, **$335.00 – 345.00**; large tab handled reamer, pink, **$45.00 – 48.00**.

Row #2 White, **$30.00 – 38.00**; cobalt blue, **$325.00 – 335.00**; crystal, **$18.00 – 20.00**; green, **$28.00 – 30.00**.

4 CUP
Green, footed, **$55.00 – 70.00**.

PERFORATED REAMER
Green, Cat. #2954, **$45.00 – 50.00**.

REFRIGERATOR WARE
BUTTER DISHES

Hazel-Atlas 1 lb. butter dishes helpfully had "Butter Cover" embossed into the tops, one would presume so people would know the larger section was meant to be the top and not the bottom. The handy grips at both ends are rectangular protrusions, not the scallops or ridges of other companies.

BLACK DOTS
Oblong, 1 lb., Cat. #2013 and 2013½, **$150.00 – 165.00.**

FAIRMONT'S BETTER BUTTER – $45.00 – 55.00.
SOUTHWEST DECORATED BUTTER DISH – $55.00 – 60.00.

BUTTER, 1 LB.
Cat. #2013 and 2013½, oblong.
Opal, **$45.00 – 50.00.**
Ritz Blue , **$300.00 – 325.00.**

REFRIGERATOR DISHES

These were originally advertised for use as individual containers or to be used stacked in sets to save room in the refrigerator. The flat cover stacking sets have either a straight line '"handy grip" set down in a well or a knob handle down in that well aperture. (See pg. 119, Ritz Blue round bowl). We believe the straight line to have been the first type made, with the knob version being a later improvement.

Notice the 1927 Butler Brother's advertising page shown on pg. 120 The entire ad is a delightful mix of Hazel-Atlas kitchenware opal products of the time. The "handy grip" line of glass is certainly visible.

DOTS
Cat. #2015½, 4½" x 5",
Red, **$35.00 – 40.00.**
Yellow with plain bottom, **$35.00 – 40.00.**

DOTS
Round drippings jar with lid, Cat. #0-3060, **$65.00 – 70.00.**

Oblong refrigerator bowl with flat cover, 4½" x 5",
Cat. #2015 & 2015½ for lid, **$35.00 – 40.00.**

REFRIGERATOR WARE
REFRIGERATOR DISHES

STACKED SET
Cat. #2015, 4½" x 5" each.
Ritz blue, **$60.00 – 70.00.**
Green, **$30.00 – 35.00.**
Yellow, **$40.00 – 45.00.**
Pink, **$40.00 – 45.00.**

PLATONITE BLACK FLORAL
Round refrigerator bowl with knob cover, 5¾",
Cat. #759; & #759½, **$25.00 – 30.00.**

PLATONITE PLAIN
Round refrigerator bowl with knob cover,
5¾", Cat. #759 & #759½, **$15.00 – 18.00.**

PLATONITE WITH RED BAND AT RIM
Round refrigerator bowl with knob cover,
5¾", Cat. #759 & 759½, **$22.00 – 25.00.**

UTILITY JAR
Rectangular, tall, 4⅛"h x 3"l,
with clear lid, **$6.00 – 8.00.**

FAIRMONT'S BETTER "PATTY ROLL"
BUTTER – Platonite, **$45.00 – 50.00.**

PLATONITE
Red band with encompassing
Red hairline decoration.
Round, 5", **$12.00 – 15.00.**
With cover, **$22.00 – 25.00.**

GREEN BAND AT RIM
Platonite, Cat. #0-759, 6", **$22.00 – 25.00.**

REFRIGERATOR WARE
REFRIGERATOR DISHES

UTILITY JAR LIDS
Ships design, "Drippings," $20.00 – 22.00 each.
Also came in plain opal, $17.00 – 20.00.

"SKATING DUTCH"
5" large cottage cheese dish, $14.00 – 15.00.
Called utility bowl if it has covers, 6", $30.00 – 35.00.

ROUND REFRIGERATOR BOWL
With flat cover, Cat. #759 bowl,
#752½ cover,
Pink, $30.00 – 35.00.

ROUND REFRIGERATOR BOWL
With flat cover, Cat. #759 bowl, #752½ cover,
Ritz blue, $70.00 – 75.00.
Green, $30.00 – 35.00.

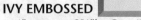

IVY EMBOSSED
4" square, 2⅝"h, Cat. #629 & 630, $6.00 – 8.00.

Not shown:
4" x 8" rectangle, 3³⁄₃₂"h, Cat. #631 & 632, $8.00 – 10.00.
¼ lb. covered butter dish, 2⁷⁄₃₂"h, Cat. #627 & 628, $10.00 – 12.00.

UTILITY JAR
Rectangular, tall, 4⅛"h x 3"h, with opal lid, $8.00 – 10.00.
Shorter, longer rectangular version, harder to find $12.00 – 15.00.

REFRIGERATOR WARE
REFRIGERATOR DISHES

Refrigerator Set
Clear pressed glass, consisting of three 5¾-inch jars, 2½ inches high. One jar acts as a cover for the one below, the top jar having a handled cover. Saves space in the refrigerator or ice box. You can see the contents at a glance. Weight, packed, 9 lbs.
35K6102 .....55c

FROM *SEARS ROEBUCK AND CO. CATALOG, 1928.*

OPAL GLASSWARE
Is The LATEST In KITCHENWARE
Pure White .. Heavy Pressed .. Opaque .. Smooth Finish!!

A complete line of kitchenware—especially adapted to kitchen use because it is PURE WHITE . . . it is SANITARY . . . and it is DURABLE. Made under an extremely high temperature to produce strength and toughness—a mighty important feature. Keep pace with department and syndicate stores by offering this new, attractive line now. IT'S A POPULAR PRICED LINE that will appeal to every housewife who sees it in your store.

SALTS—PEPPERS
(A) 4½ in., aluminum top, green lettering.
5OR-3351 — 2 doz in carton, 17 lbs
Doz .89

BUTTER JARS
(B) 1 lb., 6¾ x3¼ in.
5OR-3355 — 2 doz in carton, 38 lbs
Doz 1.25

SQUARE JARS
(C) 1 lb., 6 x 4½ x 2 in.
5OR-3354—3 doz in carton, 56 lbs.
Doz 1.05

MILK PITCHERS
(D) 20 oz., 5 in.
5OR-3356 — 2 doz in carton, 35 lbs.
Doz 1.10

EXTRACTOR SETS
(E) 2-pc. sets, 1 pt. graduated pitcher, 6 in. perforated reamer.
5OR-3365—1 doz sets in carton, 24 lbs
Doz sets 1.75

ROUND JARS
(F) 5x2½ in., recessed cover, for refrigerator.
5OR-3353 — 3 doz in carton, 35 lbs
Doz .92

MEASURING CUPS
(G) 3½ in., 8 oz., graduated in ounces and cups.
5OR-3350 — 2 doz in carton, 18 lbs
Doz .82

JUICE EXTRACTORS
(H) 6 in., sharp cone with seed retainer guard.
5OR-3352 — 3 doz in carton, 48 lbs.
Doz .95

MIXING BOWLS
(J) 8 in. diameter, extra deep shape.
5OR-3362 — 2 doz in carton, 45 lbs
Doz 1.45

MIXING BOWLS
(K) 7 in. diameter, extra deep shape.
5OR-3361 — 3 doz in carton, 48 lbs
Doz 1.10

MIXING BOWLS
(L) 6 in. diameter, extra deep shape.
5OR-3360 — 3 doz in carton, 45 lbs
Doz .80

4 PIECE RANGE SETS
(M) 4 shakers 4¾ in., aluminum tops, green lettering, each set in box.
5OR-3367—½ doz sets in pkg., 18 lbs
Doz sets 3.95

5-PC. BOWL SETS
(N) 5, 6, 7, 8 and 9 in. mixing bowls nested.
5OR-3370 — 1 set in carton, 10 lbs
Set .75

7 PIECE KITCHEN SETS
(P) Set consists of: 4½ in. salt & pepper shakers, 1 lb. square refrigerator jar, 8 in. mixing bowl, 9 in. mixing bowl, 16 oz. graduated pitcher, 6 in. perforated reamer.
5OR-3371 — 1 set in carton, 15 lbs.
Set .75

7-Pc. Kitchen Sets

"PLATONITE" PURE WHITE GLASSWARE

With smooth edges and a fire polished finish. Made under an extremely high temperature to produce toughness, strength and heat resisting qualities "Platonite" is hard to break—it will not craze! Demonstrate its unusual durability to your customers—tell them the CUP IS ALL ONE PIECE.

BUTLER BROTHERS

NOTICE THE 2-LB. BUTTER JAR IS UPSIDE DOWN IN THIS 1927 BUTLER BROTHERS AD.

SHAKERS

Kitchen shakers made by Hazel-Atlas are desired for their numerous designs. Hazel-Atlas range shakers are found in two basic shapes: round with ribs and square. We have divided each of these shapes into patterns using known designations from collectors. In some cases, no consistent names have been forthcoming; so we have simply presented a terminology in order for collectors to know what particular shakers are being discussed in ads or auctions.

Most designs were established by Hazel-Atlas but some were designated by decorating firms Gay Fad and Tipp Novelty Company. Many Hazel-Atlas shakers are marked with the familiar "H" over "A" on the bottom, but some are not.

Confusion still exists between the square shakers of McKee and those of Hazel-Atlas. Hazel-Atlas square shakers have a distinct sharp edge down the corners, whereas McKee shakers have less sharp, more rounded edges. The screw threads on top of Hazel-Atlas shakers are immediately on top of the squared design, but McKee shakers have a rounded shoulder before the threads are encountered. This should help distinguish between the two if the shakers are not marked.

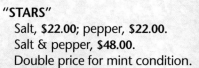

"STARS"
Salt, **$22.00**; pepper, **$22.00**.
Salt & pepper, **$48.00**.
Double price for mint condition.

ROOSTERS – Gay Fad Studios Design. c. 1954. Salt, **$22.00**; pepper, **$22.00**; salt & pepper, **$45.00**; flour, **$25.00**; sugar, **$25.00**; set of four, **$100.00**. SEE MATCHING CRUET ON PAGE 81.

SHAKERS
ROUND RIBBED

FIRED-ON – Salt, green, $30.00; pepper, pastel green, $35.00; flour, yellow, $35.00; salt, pink, $35.00; pepper, green, $30.00.

FIRED-ON RED – Salt, $30.00; pepper, $30.00; salt & pepper, $65.00; flour, $30.00; sugar, $30.00; set of four, $130.00.

ARROWS – Blue or red, salt, $35.00; pepper, $20.00.

BOLD STRIPE DECORATED RED
Salt, $32.00; pepper, $30.00; salt & pepper, $65.00.

SHAKERS
ROUND RIBBED

OLD ENGLISH DECORATED RED
Salt, $32.00; pepper, $30.00; salt & pepper, $65.00.

RED STRIPES – Salt, $25.00; pepper, $20.00; flour, $33.00; sugar, $33.00; set of four, $120.00.

GREEN STRIPES – Salt, $25.00; pepper, $20.00; salt & pepper, $48.00; flour, $33.00; sugar, $33.00; set of four, $120.00.

ROUND RIBBED PLATONITE

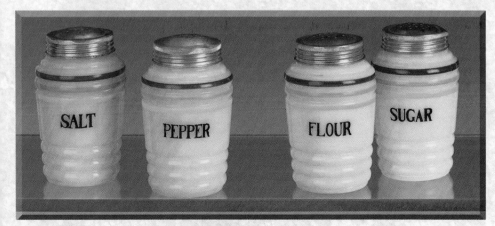

RED/YELLOW STRIPE – Salt, $35.00; pepper, $35.00; salt & pepper, $75.00; flour, $35.00; sugar, $35.00; set of four, $150.00.

SHAKERS
ROUND RIBBED PLATONITE

BLACK LETTERS – Salt, **$18.00**; pepper, **$18.00**; salt & pepper, **$40.00**; flour, **$24.00**; sugar, **$24.00**; set of four, **$90.00**.

REPRODUCTION FROM CHINA – Made in China exclusively for Heart & Home Collectables, **New, no price available.**

COLONIAL COUPLE – **$35.00.**

SCRIPTED LETTERS LARGE – Salt, **$22.00**; pepper, **$22.00**; salt & pepper, **$45.00**; flour, **$25.00**; sugar, **$25.00**; set of four, **$100.00**.

SCRIPTED LETTERS SMALL – Ginger, **$18.00**; cloves, **$18.00**; paprika, **$18.00**; pepper, **$16.00**.

SCRIPTED LETTERS, SMALL SPICES – cinnamon, **$18.00**; nutmeg, **$18.00**; celery salt, **$18.00**.

SHAKERS
SQUARE

DUTCH FIRED-ON COLORS – Small on stand, 3⅛", salt, $25.00; pepper, $25.00; salt & pepper, $55.00; flour, $35.00; sugar, $35.00; set of four, $125.00; set of four on stand, $145.00.

DUTCH – 3⅜", salt, $20.00; pepper, $20.00; salt & pepper, $45.00; flour, $25.00; sugar, $25.00; set of four, $110.00; set of four on stand, $125.00.

WINDMILLS – Large, 4½", salt, $30.00; pepper, $30.00; salt & pepper, $65.00. Small, 3⅛", salt (not shown), $22.00; pepper, $22.00; salt & pepper, $45.00.

FROM *GLASSWARE BY HAZEL-ATLAS* **1957 CATALOG, PAGE 31.**

DUTCH FIRED-ON COLORS – Large, 4½", salt, $45.00; pepper, $45.00; salt & pepper, $95.00; flour, $60.00; sugar, $60.00; set of four, $225.00.

DUTCH FIRED-ON COLORS – Small narrow, 3⅜", salt, $25.00; pepper (not shown), $25.00; salt & pepper, $55.00; flour, $35.00; sugar (not shown), $35.00; set of four, $125.00.

SHAKERS
SQUARE

DUTCH SMALL – 3⅛", salt, $20.00; pepper, $20.00; salt & pepper, $45.00.

DUTCH LARGE – 4½", salt, $25.00; pepper, $25.00; salt & pepper, $55.00.

DUTCH SMALL NARROW – 3⅜", salt, $20.00; pepper, $20.00; salt & pepper, $45.00; with stand, $60.00.

DUTCH SKATERS RED – Salt, $30.00; pepper, $30.00; salt & pepper, $65.00; flour, $35.00; sugar, $35.00; set of four, $140.00; **DUTCH SKATERS, GREEN OR BLUE** – salt, green, $30.00; pepper, green, $30.00; salt & pepper, green, $65.00; flour, blue, $35.00; sugar, blue, $35.00; set of four, $140.00.

SHAKERS
SQUARE

DECO – Salt, **$65.00**; pepper, **$65.00**; salt & pepper, **$135.00**; flour, **$65.00**; sugar, **$65.00**; set of four, **$275.00**.

ELECTROCHEF OR EMBOSSED HOT POINT
Salt, **$20.00**; pepper, **$20.00**; salt & pepper, **$42.00**; flour, **$26.00**; sugar, **$26.00**; set of four, **$100.00**.

IVY GREEN – Salt, **$60.00**; pepper, **$60.00**; salt & pepper, **$125.00**; **IVY DARK GREEN** – salt (not shown), **$60.00**; pepper, **$60.00**; salt & pepper, **$125.00**.

FIRED-ON BLACK – Salt, **$25.00**; **FIRED-ON YELLOW** – pepper, **$25.00**; **FIRED-ON GREEN** – sugar, **$25.00**; set of four, **$110.00**; **FIRED-ON BLACK** – salt, **$25.00**; pepper, **$25.00**; salt & pepper, **$55.00**; **FIRED-ON BEIGE** – flour (not shown), **$25.00**.

SHAKERS
SQUARE

VERTICAL LINES, RED – Salt, $30.00; pepper, $30.00; salt & pepper, $65.00; flour, $40.00; sugar, $40.00; set of four, $150.00.

VERTICAL LINES, GREEN – Salt, $35.00; pepper, $35.00; salt & pepper, $75.00.

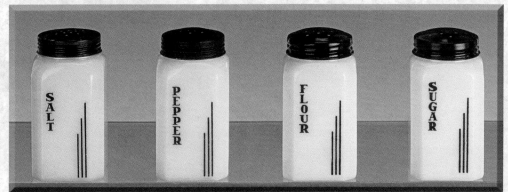

VERTICAL LINES, BLACK – Salt, $30.00; pepper, $30.00; salt & pepper, $65.00; flour, $40.00; sugar, $40.00; set of four, $150.00.

ROUND & TALL RIBBED

CONCENTRIC RIBBED, TALL – Green, $10.00 ea., $22.00 pair;

VERTICAL RIBBED, ROUND – Blue, $12.00 each; $25.00 pair; yellow, $12.00 ea., $26.00 pair; red, $10.00 ea., $22.00 pair.

SHAKERS
SQUARE

ROSEMALING OR "DUTCH TULIPS"
Gay Fad Studios Designs
Large yellow – salt, **$40.00**; sugar, **$40.00**;
allspice, **$40.00**; cloves, **$40.00**; oil, **$40.00**;
large red – pepper, **$45.00**; cinnamon, **$45.00**;
nutmeg, **$45.00**; small red – pepper, **$40.00**.

PENNSYLVANIA DUTCH SYMBOL
Salt, **$25.00**; pepper, **$25.00**; salt & pepper, **$50.00**;
Roastmeat seasoning, two styles, **$30.00 ea.**

ROUND & TALL RIBBED

CONCENTRIC RIBBED, TALL – Yellow, **$10.00 ea.**, **$22.00 pr.**;

VERTICAL RIBBED, ROUND – Green, **$10.00 ea.**, **$22.00 pr.**; crystal, **$5.00 ea.**, **$10.00 pr.**

SHAKERS
SQUARE

SHIELD, BLACK – Salt, **$18.00**; pepper, **$18.00**; salt & pepper, **$38.00**; flour, **$22.00**; sugar, **$22.00**; set of four, **$85.00**.

SHIELD, GREEN – Salt, **$18.00**; pepper, **$18.00**; salt & pepper, **$38.00**.

SHIELD WITH BLUE OR RED DOTS – Salt, **$60.00**; pepper, **$60.00**; salt & pepper, **$125.00**; flour, **$95.00**; sugar, **$95.00**; set of four, **$325.00**.

SHAKERS
SQUARE

EMBOSSED TRANSPARENT, PINK – Salt, $60.00; pepper, $60.00; salt & pepper, $125.00.

EMBOSSED TRANSPARENT, CRYSTAL – salt (not shown), $30.00; pepper, $30.00; salt & pepper, $65.00.

EMBOSSED TRANSPARENT, GREEN – Salt, $60.00; pepper, $60.00; salt & pepper, $125.00; flour, $90.00; sugar, $90.00; set of four, $325.00.

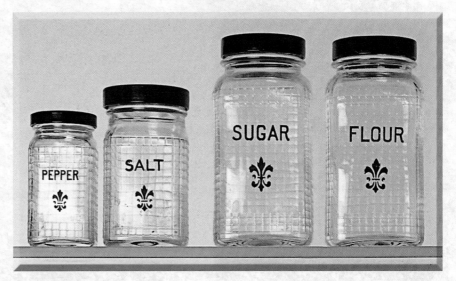

SQUARE BLOCK, FLEUR DE LIS – Small, 8 oz., salt (not shown), $14.00; pepper, $14.00; salt & pepper, $30.00; medium, 16 oz., salt, $18.00; pepper (not shown), $18.00; salt & pepper, $40.00; large, 20 oz., flour, $35.00 – 38.00; sugar, $35.00 – 38.00.

BLOCK "SQUARES" DESIGN
Plain (no lettering). Had label with food product. Small, $5.00; with label, $15.00; large, $15.00; with label, $25.00.

SHAKERS
TABLE

...ow are various types of table shakers which Hazel-Atlas made for direct sales or as product container shakers for ...panies. The #3530 Concentric Rings type shakers were in their line at least from 1939 onward. We know they were sold ...y F. W. Woolworth's and generally sported the moisture proof lids which had a white moisture absorbing disc and a covering ring of red, blue, green, or yellow, atop an aluminum cone screw type lid. The shaker lids were made by Airko and another example of these can be found under the pattern Starlight on page 216. Their #30 line of bubbled squares has probably graced the table in a restaurant you frequent.

Restaurant and Institutional Ware by HAZEL-ATLAS

477-8—1 oz. Salt & Pepper
Shaker—Nickel Pltd. Brass Tops
Pkd. 6 doz. ctn. Wt. 13 lbs.
Height 3⁵⁄₁₆" Top ⅞"

30—1⅝ oz. Salt & Pepper
Shaker—Aluminum Tops
Pkd. 6 doz. ctn. Wt. 14 lbs.
Height 3⁵⁄₃₂" Top 1¼"

1533—¾ oz. Salt & Pepper
Shaker—Nickel Pltd. Brass Tops
Pkd. 6 doz. ctn. Wt. 9 lbs.
Height 2²⁹⁄₃₂" Top ¾"

1038—2¾ oz. Barrel
Salt and Pepper
Shaker—Tin Tops, Red Coated
Pkd. 6 doz. ctn. Wt. 15 lbs.
Height 3" Top 2"

477-4—1 oz. Salt & Pepper
Shaker—Stainless Steel Caps
Pkd. 6 doz. ctn. Wt. 13 lbs.
Height 3⅛" Top ⅞"

2442—2 oz. Salt & Pepper
Shaker—Stainless Steel Caps
Pkd. 6 doz. ctn. Wt. 19 lbs.
Height 3½" Top 1⁵⁄₃₂"

4231—3 oz. Salt & Pepper
Shaker—Stainless Steel Caps
Pkd. 6 doz. ctn. Wt. 27 lbs.
Height 4⅜" Top 1⁵⁄₃₂"

5053—4 oz. Salt & Pepper
Shaker—Stainless Steel Caps
Pkd. 2 doz. ctn. Wt. 8 lbs.
Height 3¹⁵⁄₃₂" Top 1¾"

5053-410—4 oz. Sugar Server
Stainless Steel Cap
Self-closing spout
Pkd. 2 doz. ctn. Wt. 9 lbs.
Height 3¹⁵⁄₃₂" Top 1¾"

5053-710—4 oz. Cream Server
(Ketchup or Mustard Server)
Stainless Steel Cap
Pkd. 2 doz. ctn. Wt. 9 lbs.
Height 3¹⁵⁄₃₂" Top 1¾"

5052-970—12 oz. Sugar Server
Stainless Steel Cap
Center hole
Pkd. 2 doz. ctn. Wt. 20 lbs.
Height 5¾" Top 2⅜"

5052-920—12 oz. Sugar Server
Stainless Steel Cap
Self-closing spout
Pkd. 2 doz. ctn. Wt. 20 lbs.
Height 5¾" Top 2⅜"

†Item numbers within ( ) in light face type are the former numbers

21

FROM *GLASSWARE BY HAZEL-ATLAS CATALOG*, 1957, PAGE 21.

SHAKERS
TABLE

477-7—1 oz. Salt & Pepper
Shaker—Molded Tops—Red
Pkd. 6 doz. ctn. Wt. 12 lbs.
Height 3$\frac{7}{16}$" Top $\frac{7}{8}$"

"LIGHTHOUSE" SHAKER
$10.00 – 12.00.

"CONCENTRIC RIBS"
3½"h, flat, 2½ oz., marked HA96292,
aluminum lids, with clover & tulip
embossing, $15.00 – 18.00 pair.

"CONCENTRIC RINGS"
Opal, 3½"h, footed, 1 oz.,
Cat. #3530, $8.00 – 10.00 pair.

"ICICLE"
3½"h, Cat. #468,
Green, $15.00 each.

Not shown:
Crystal, $8.00 each.

"INDENTED PANELS"
$10.00 – 12.00.

SHAKERS
TABLE

"MODERNISTIC DECO"
Green, 2½"h, $17.50 each.

"PAPERCLIP"
2⅞"h, $15.00 each.

COLORED RINGS
3½"h, marked HA, $8.00 each.

DUTCH WINDMILL
Silver Sea black pepper label, $20.00 each.
$25.00 with label.

FLASHED COLOR
Sloped sides, 3⅛"h,
Marked HA 5, $10.00 – 12.00 pair.

SHAKERS
TABLE

**CHASE CANDY CO. ARMSTRONG CAKE
DECORATING TRIM-ETTES**
  Crystal, 3¼"h, marked #4894 K-8.
  $3.00 – 4.00 each, $6.00 – 8.00 with label.

CRYSTAL
  2⅝"h, Cat. #1533,
  3 oz., **$6.00 – 8.00 pair.**

  Not shown:
    Pink, **$15.00 – 18.00 each.**
    Green, **$15.00 – 18.00 each.**

FROST DECORATED PINK
  3½"h, marked HA 2 -8, **$20.00 – 25.00 pair.**

PINK
3¼"h Cat. #477, **$6.00 – 7.00.**

STICKNEY AND POOR'S PAPRIKA
  Crystal, 1½ oz., 3½"
  Cat. #2442, **$6.00 – 8.00 with label.**

SHAKERS
TABLE

GREEN STRING DECORATION
3¼"h, Cat. #477-5, **$8.00 – 10.00 pair.**

RITZ BLUE
2²⁹⁄₃₂"h, ¾ oz., Cat. #1533, **$25.00 each.**

CRYSTAL
3¼"h, marked HA2-K489,
$6.00 – 8.00 pair.

BARREL
Aster nutmeg. Kroger mustard also
came in a barrel jar. **$12.50 – 15.00.**

OCCASIONAL DISHES

LEAF CANDY TRAY
8" point to point, Cat. #276, **$7.00 – 9.00.**

LEAF COASTER
With gold rim and label, Cat. #475, Dec. #670, **$4.00 – 5.00.**

LEAF CELERY
9¾", Cat. #279, sold in sets of five as "lazy susan," **$4.00 – 5.00.**

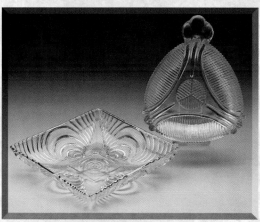

LEAF SILVER OVERLAY
Partitioned dish, Cat. #191, **$10.00 – 12.00.**

PRESERVE DISH
6", handled, Cat. #577, crystal, **$6.00 – 8.00.**

Not shown:
Pink, **$10.00 – 12.00.**

"SOUNDWAVE"
Candy plate, 8⅜", square, Cat. #574, **$6.00 – 8.00.**

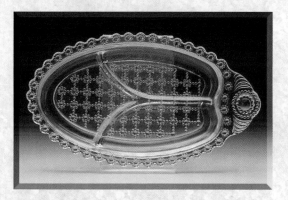

"JEWEL"
Divided relish, 10¼" x 5¾"w, Cat. #129, Crystal, **$12.00 – 15.00.**

"PRISM"– 6⅜", amethyst, square, **$10.00 – 12.00.**

"STRAWBERRY"
6¹⁄₁₆" x 6¹³⁄₁₆", Cat. #639.
Crystal, **$4.00 – 5.00.**
Opaque, Cat. #0-691, **$3.00 – 4.00.**

"TEARDROP"
Four-toe, mint, 6⅜", Cat. #130.
Crystal, **$4.00 – 5.00.**

OPAQUE WARE

See Also, Snack Sets, page 141, Embossed Floral Design, page 157, and Vases & Flowerpots, page 142.

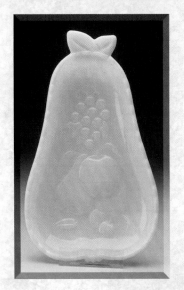

BLOSSOM PATTERN
Pear dish, 4⅜" x 8⅛",
Cat. #0-641, **$4.00 – 6.00.**

"CUBE"
Creamer/sugar, footed,
Cat. #0-333 & #0-334, **$2.00 – 3.00 each.**

"DIAMOND SQUARES"
Candy dish, 6⅞", Cat. #0-281, **$3.00 – 4.00.**

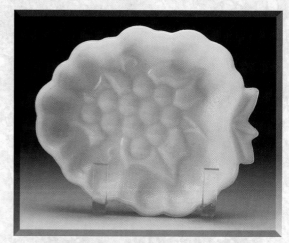

HEN-ON-NEST
  3½", Cat. #0-1717 & #0-1718, **$6.00 – 8.00.**

GRAPE DISH
  5¹¹⁄₁₆" x 7", Cat. #0-692, **$5.00 – 6.00.**

LACE EDGE PLATE
  Cat. # 0-9644, **$4.00 – 5.00.**
  With decoration, **$8.00 – 10.00.**
  Also made in Ritz Blue, **$25.00 – 30.00.**

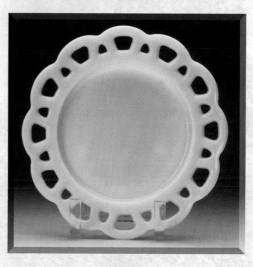

PEBBLED SURFACE BOWL
  Crimped edge, 7½", **$8.00 – 10.00.**

BUFFET TRAY WITH CARAMEL COLORED LEAVES – 5 pieces plus stand, $20.00 – 25.00.

MODERNTONE
Lazy susan relish tray with salad bowls and frost tongs, $25.00 – 28.00.

ALSO MADE WITH BLACK FROST DECORATION ON BLACK BASE WHICH WAS MARKETED AS "MID-NITE MAGIC."

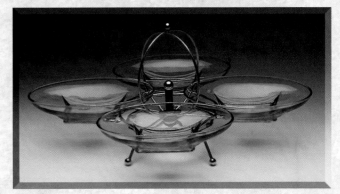

CAPRI BLUE
Buffet server, 4 piece with stand, $35.00 – 40.00.

LEAF CELERY DISH
The long celery occasional dish was sold in groups of five and termed a "lazy susan." 4⅜" x 9¹¹⁄₁₆", 22K gold eagle. $20.00 – 25.00.

THIS ITEM IS ALSO SHOWN ON PAGE 137.

DAISY IN GRANADA GOLD COLOR
$4.00 – 6.00 each.

**BLOSSOM PATTERN FRONT/
INFORMAL PATTERN BACK**
Cup and plate, $6.00 – 8.00.

SAVOY TV SET
   Part of Orchard line, $8.00 – 10.00 each.

Not shown:
   Crystal with colored edge trims.

SNACK, SIP & SMOKE SET
   Cat. #1305, $4.00 – 5.00 set.

THIS SET WAS SOLD TWO WAYS: AS A LUNCHEON PARTY SET AND AS A COCKTAIL
PARTY SET. ONE CORNER OF THE TRAY HAS AN INDENT FOR A CIGARETTE.

Vases & Flowerpots

EARLY AMERICAN STYLE
2⅜"h x 3³⁄₁₆", ruffled rim flowerpot, $6.00 – 8.00.

INSIDE LABEL

FLASHED COLORS – 3⅝", $8.00 – 10.00 each.
Not shown: Blue

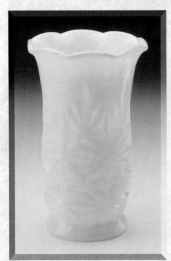

RUFFLED VASE
Tumbler type, 5¾" x 3½"w,
Cat. #0311, $7.00 – 8.00 each.

RUFFLED VASE
Ribbed middle, tumbler type,
6¾"h x 4¼"w, Cat. #0-1102,
$8.00 – 10.00 each.

RUFFLED VASE
Pyramids, Tumbler type,
5¾"h x 3⅝"w, $8.00 – 9.00.

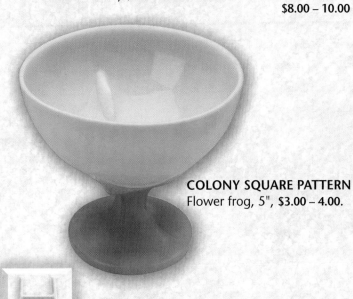

COLONY SQUARE PATTERN
Flower frog, 5", $3.00 – 4.00.

BUD VASE
9", 8 panel top, prism pattern,
Cat. #4043, $4.00 – 5.00.

COLORS – COBALT BLUE, PINK, GREEN, AND CRYSTAL

A few pieces of Aurora have been found in pink, and these fetch a price comparable to the blue due to their scarcity. The small bowl, creamer, and tumbler have, so far, never been found in pink. Several Canadian readers report pink and green are more readily found there than in the States.

Both green and crystal cereal bowls, cups, and saucers have been found. Of course, blue is the color most desired, but that is beginning to be a problem with the lack of deep utility bowls being found.

UTILITY BOWL
Cat. #9642, 4½"w x 2⅜"h, $65.00.

COBALT OR PINK		GREEN	
① Bowl, 4½"w, x 2⅜"h, Cat. #9642	$65.00	Bowl, 5⅜", cereal	$8.00
② Bowl, 5⅜", cereal	$18.00	Cup	$8.00
⑤ Creamer, 4½", milk	$25.00	Saucer	$2.50
③ Cup	$18.00	**CRYSTAL**	
Plate, 6½"	$14.00	Bowl, 5⅜", cereal	$5.00
⑥ Saucer	$4.00	Bowl, 4½", utility, 2⅜" deep	$15.00
④ Tumbler, 4¾", 10 oz.,	$26.00		

"BEEHIVE"
COLORS – CRYSTAL, PINK, AND PLATONITE

To date, most of what has brought any notice to the "Beehive" pattern in Depression ware circles were the large, footed tea tumblers and pitchers. They have been collectible in their own right for 30 years. We only know of the sugar and creamer being found in Platonite (valued at $8.00 each).

SUGAR
Cat. #352-352½, 11 oz., with lid, **$10.00.**

	CRYSTAL	PINK		CRYSTAL	PINK
① Bowl, 4⅞", berry, 2 hdld.	$3.00	$5.00	⑦ Sherbet, 3¾", flat	$6.00	$8.00
② Bowl, 8⅝" berry, 2 hdld.	$10.00	$14.00	⑧ Sugar, 11½ oz.	$5.00	$8.00
③ Bowl, 19¾ oz., utility, Cat. #355	$12.50	$17.50	Sugar lid	$4.00	$5.00
Butter and cover, 6", Cat. #355 & ½	$25.00	$35.00	⑩ Tray, 12¼", serving	$12.00	$15.00
④ Creamer, 9½ oz., Cat. #351	$5.50	$8.00	Tumbler, 9 oz., flat		$22.50
Cup	$8.00	$8.00	⑤ Tumbler, 15 oz., ftd. tea	$8.00	$12.50
⑥ Pitcher, 84 oz., with ice lip	$25.00	$45.00			

CANDY STRIPE – 1950s
COLORS – PLATONITE WITH BROWN, RED, TURQUOISE OR YELLOW STRIPES

This pattern is mostly collected in red stripes, but it can be found in the colors listed above. Other colors may exist, but this is all we have seen. Let me know if there are others. Red seems popular on the Internet; but it needs to be good color and not faded from repeated dishwasher use to be collectible.

BOWL
4⅞", $10.00.

CUP – $9.00.
SAUCER
5⅜", $2.00.

TUMBLER
5⅛", 10 oz., $12.50.

MUG
8 oz., $12.00.

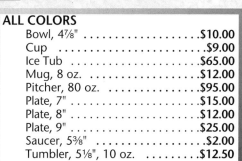

ALL COLORS
Bowl, 4⅞"	$10.00
Cup	$9.00
Ice Tub	$65.00
Mug, 8 oz.	$12.00
Pitcher, 80 oz.	$95.00
Plate, 7"	$15.00
Plate, 8"	$12.00
Plate, 9"	$25.00
Saucer, 5⅜"	$2.00
Tumbler, 5⅛", 10 oz.	$12.50

CAPRI COLONY & COLONY SQUARE

Capri refers to the blue color of this ware. This electric blue coloring was popular in the 1960s and can be seen in wares from other companies as well. The Colony name comes from actual labels on the square based items; square, hexagonal, and octagonal are descriptions coming from the shapes. Shape names seemed to be the only easy way to describe these. The square-based tumbler is the only item that will fit the square indention plate. There may be a square-based cup, but I haven't seen one.

Ashtray, 3½", square, embossed flower $10.00	㉝ Candy jar, with cover, footed. $32.00	
㉜ Bowl, 7¾", oval $15.00	㉖ Chip and dip, 2 bowls	
㉚ Bowl, 5¾", square, deep $10.00	(8¾" and 4¾" on metal rack) $25.00	
Bowl, 9⅛" x 3" high $25.00	㉙ Plate, 8", square $8.00	
Bowl, 9½" x 2⅞" high $22.00	㉟ Plate, 8", square, with square cup rest $8.00	
㉗ Bowl, 4¾", square $6.00	㉘ Plate, 8⅞", square $10.00	
㉛ Bowl, 7¾", rectangular $14.00	Plate, 8⅞", square snack, with round cup rest $8.00	
Bowl, 6", round, sq. bottom $7.00	Saucer, 5½", square $1.00	
Bowl, 10¾", salad $24.00	㉞ Tumbler, 4¼", 9 oz. $7.50	

CAPRI DAISY

A nesting ashtray set was also made in this design and is pictured on page 10. We've seen crystal ones – have you seen any in Capri?

⑤	Bowl, 6", round	$10.00
③	Bowl, 9½", round	$25.00
①	Cup, round	$7.00
②	Plate, 9½", round, snack with cup rest	$9.50
④	Saucer, 6", round	$1.00

CAPRI HOBNAIL

⑫ Bowl, 5⅜", salad, round	$7.00	④ Saucer, 6", round	$1.00
⑬ Creamer, round	$12.50	⑧ Sugar, round	$8.00
⑥ Cup, round	$4.00	⑦ Sugar lid	$12.00
⑩ Plate, 7¼", salad	$6.00	⑨ Tidbit, 3-tier (round 9⅞" plate,	
⑪ Plate, 9⅞", dinner, round	$8.00	7⅛" plate, 6" saucer)	$22.50

CAPRI OCTAGON

CUP – $4.00.

PLATE
7¼", salad, **$6.00.**

PLATE
9¾", dinner, **$9.00.**

SAUCER – $1.00.

Not shown:
Bowl, 4¾", **$7.00.**
Bread and butter plate, 5¾", **$4.00.**

CAPRI SKOL

Skol is a Swedish toasting phrase meaning "to your health," and perhaps that's what this name implied.

㉕ Bowl, 4⅞", round $5.00	㉒ Tumbler, 3¼", 8 oz., old fashioned $8.00
⑥ Cup, round $4.00	⑲ Tumbler, 3⅝", 6 oz. $5.00
④ Saucer, 6", round $1.00	⑳ Tumbler, 4" $4.00
㉓ Sherbet, 2¾" high, round footed $5.00	Tumbler, 5¼" $5.00
㉔ Tumbler, 3", 3 oz., sham bottom, cocktail ..$4.00	Tumbler, 6", 10 oz. $7.00
⑱ Tumbler, 3", 4 oz., fruit $4.00	㉑ Vase, 8" $20.00

CAPRI SWIRL

㉗ Bowl, 4¾" $6.00	Cup, round $4.00
㉘ Bowl, 8¾" $12.00	Plate, 10", snack, fan shaped with cup rest $7.00
㉖ Chip and dip, 2 bowls	Tumbler, 5½", 12 oz., tea $10.00
(8¾" and 4¾" on metal rack) $25.00	Vase, 8½", ruffled $35.00

CAPRI SWIRL COLONIAL

Bowl, 5 5/88" $8.00	Tumbler, 3 1/16" $8.00
(39) Bowl, 6 1/16", round $7.00	(40) Tumbler, 5", 12 oz. $10.00
(1) Cup, round $7.00	(41) Tumbler, 2¾", 4 oz. $7.00
(13) Creamer, round $12.50	(36) Tumbler, 3 1/16" $8.00
(38) Plate, 7⅛", round, salad $7.00	(37) Tumbler, 4¼", 9 oz. $7.50
Plate, 7", salad, round $7.00	

ALSO AVAILABLE IN CAPRI

Ashtray, 3¼", triangular $6.00	Stem, 5½", water, six-sided base $9.00
Ashtray, 3¼", round $6.00	Tumbler, 3", 5 oz., pentagonal bottom $7.00
Ashtray, 5", round $8.00	Tumbler, 3⅛", 5 oz., pentagonal $7.00
Ashtray, 6⅝", triangular $12.00	Tumbler, 4¼", 9 oz., water, pentagonal bottom $7.50
Bowl, 9½" oval 1½" high $9.00	Tumbler, 5", 12 oz., tea, pentagonal bottom $10.00
Stem, 4½", sherbet, six-sided base $7.50	

CHECKERBOARD – 1930s
COLORS – CRYSTAL, GREEN AND IRIDESCENT

Checkerboard seems to be rare in crystal, but it is not often sought in that color. Carnival collectors used to seek the iridescent.Green is the most collected color. Note the 5¾" scalloped bowl which is only half iridized.

IRIDIZED ORANGE
Plate, 8" with windmill, $15.00.
Butter dish with lid, $30.00.

IRIDIZED BOWL
5¾", scalloped, half iridized, $35.00.

GREEN AND IRIDESCENT
① Ashtray, 4", with match holder .$13.00
② Ashtray, 5¾", with match holder,
    Cat. #758 . . . .$15.00
③ Bowl, 4¼", berry $8.00
④ Bowl, 5¼", tab handled soup . . .$35.00

Bowl, 5¾", scalloped, half iridized . .$35.00
⑥ Butter dish lid $20.00
   Butter bottom $10.00
   Butter with lid $30.00
⑤ Plate, 8" $15.00
* DEDUCT 20 – 25% FOR CRYSTAL

CLOVERLEAF – 1930 – 1936

COLORS – PINK, GREEN, YELLOW, CRYSTAL, AND BLACK

Cloverleaf is probably the most recognized pattern of Depression glass. Non-collectors may not know the actual name but they certainly will know it as shamrocks or clover when first seeing it displayed. Collectors of green have a wider variety of pieces to gather. It it the color in most demand. The 8" bowl and tumblers sell quickly. All bowls (in any color) as well as grill plates and tumblers are becoming more difficult to gather. There appear to be like numbers of collectors for black or yellow Cloverleaf. Few hunt pink or crystal. Besides luncheon pieces in pink, a berry bowl and a flared, 10-ounce tumbler exist. That pink tumbler was meagerly circulated and has never been found in crystal.

PINK	
Ashtray, 4", match holder in center	$60.00
② Bowl, 4", dessert	$40.00
⑤ Cup	$9.00
③ Plate, 8", luncheon	$11.00
⑥ Saucer	$3.00
④ Sherbet, 3", footed	$10.00
① Tumbler, 3¾", 10 oz., flat, flared	$30.00

CLOVERLEAF

GREEN

② Bowl, 4", dessert $40.00	⑯ Plate, 10¼", grill $25.00
⑧ Bowl, 5", cereal $50.00	⑭ Salt and pepper, pair $40.00
⑨ Bowl, 7", deep salad $80.00	⑥ Saucer $3.00
⑩ Bowl, 8" $100.00	④ Sherbet, 3", footed $12.00
⑮ Candy dish and cover $70.00	⑫ Sugar, 3⅝", footed $10.00
⑬ Creamer, 3⅝", footed $10.00	⑦ Tumbler, 4", 9 oz., flat $70.00
⑤ Cup $9.00	① Tumbler, 3¾", 10 oz., flat, flared . . .$55.00
⑪ Plate, 6", sherbet $10.00	⑰ Tumbler, 5¾", 10 oz., footed $30.00
③ Plate, 8", luncheon $8.00	

CLOVERLEAF

YELLOW

② Bowl, 4", dessert $40.00	③ Plate, 8", luncheon $14.00
⑧ Bowl, 5", cereal $60.00	⑯ Plate, 10¼", grill $28.00
⑨ Bowl, 7", deep salad $90.00	⑭ Salt and pepper, pair $135.00
⑮ Candy dish and cover $125.00	Saucer $4.00
⑬ Creamer, 3⅝", footed $22.00	④ Sherbet, 3", footed $14.00
Cup $11.00	⑫ Sugar, 3⅝", footed $22.00
⑪ Plate, 6", sherbet $10.00	⑰ Tumbler, 5¾", 10 oz., footed $42.50

BLACK

⑱ Ashtray, 4", match holder in center $60.00	③ Plate, 8", luncheon $15.00
⑲ Ashtray, 5¾", match holder in center $95.00	⑭ Salt and pepper, pair $100.00
⑬ Creamer, 3⅝", footed $16.00	⑥ Saucer $5.00
⑤ Cup $16.00	④ Sherbet, 3", footed $20.00
⑪ Plate, 6", sherbet $40.00	⑫ Sugar, 3⅝", footed $16.00

COLONIAL COUPLE
COLORS – PLATONITE WITH TRIMS

There are likely other pieces to be found in this charming ware made around 1940. Though Hazel-Atlas had first come out with a line of Platonite in the early 1930s, much of their early ware had translucent edges and was presented as white ware. Toward the late thirties and early forties when color trims were taking the glass world by storm, they started affixing various designs to their white Platonite which by now had wonderful, full white coloring and was a perfect background on which to display images of nursery rhymes, Dutch children, windmills, Hopalong Cassidy, Tom and Jerry, red birds, forget-me-nots, black and red stripes — or a "Colonial Couple."

⑤	Bowl with lid, round, refrigerator	$35.00
⑦	Bowl, 5"	$15.00
	Cup	$15.00
③	Egg cup	$22.00
④	Pitcher, 16 oz., milk	$38.00
②	Plate, dessert	$10.00
	Saucer	$5.00
⑥	Shaker, kitchen, pair	$65.00
①	Tumbler, 8 oz., flat	$20.00

"DIAMOND WITH THUMBPRINT" – 1936
COLORS – CRYSTAL AND PINK

The ball pitcher in this design is sometimes mistaken for Anchor Hocking's Waterford. This pattern has a "thumbprint" middle indentation.

CRYSTAL

⑤	Bowl, 4", berry	$5.00	④ Sherbet, 3⅞", 6 oz.		$5.00
	Bowl, 5⅛", cereal	$8.00	② Tumbler, 3⁵⁄₁₆", juice, Cat. #371		$5.00
	Bowl, 9", salad	$12.00	③ Tumbler, 5¹⁄₁₆", 9 oz. water, Cat. #372		$8.00
	Pitcher, 40 oz., ball	$15.00	① Tumbler, 5⅞", tea, footed		$8.00
	Pitcher, 80 oz., ball	$25.00	***PINK ADD 40%**		

DIAMOND OPTIC – LATE 1930s

COLORS – CRYSTAL, COBALT, GREEN, PINK

Older collectors sometimes refer to this pattern as "Quilt."

TUMBLERS
   3 oz., juice, **$7.00.**
   9 oz., Cat. #1709, 4¼", **$9.00.**
   12 oz., tea, **$15.00.**

PLATE
   8", marked "Urban's Liberty Flour," **$12.00.**

TUMBLER
   3" juice, **$7.00.**

TUMBLER
   9 oz., 4¼", Cat. #1709, **$9.00.**

CUP – **$8.00.**

SAUCER – **$2.00.**

PITCHER
   54 oz., Cat. #1876, **$35.00.**

---

*PINK/GREEN
   **Cup $8.00
   Pitcher, 54 oz., Cat. #1876 . . . .$35.00
   **Plate, 8" $6.00
   **Saucer $2.00
   Tumbler, 3", juice $7.00
   Tumbler, 4¼", 9 oz., Cat. #1709 . . . .$9.00
   Tumbler, 12 oz., tea $15.00
   *CRYSTAL 60% OF PINK/GREEN; COBALT - ADD 50%

**ITEMS MARKED URBAN'S LIBERTY FLOUR, DOUBLE PRICE LISTED

EMBOSSED FLORAL DESIGN – 1950s
COLOR – PLATONITE

This little pattern is seldom recognized, though it has an endearing quality.

PLATE
9", Cat. #0-83, **$6.00.**

PLATE
7", **$3.00.**

CUP
Cat. #0-81, **$3.00.**

Bowl, 5¼" dessert, Cat #0-272	**$3.00**
Bowl, 8" soup, Cat. # 0-271	**$7.00**
Cup, Cat. #0-81, #300	**$3.00**
Plate, 7"	**$3.00**
Plate, 9", Cat. #0-83	**$6.00**
Platter, 11", Cat. # 0-270	**$10.00**
Saucer, Cat. #0-82	**$1.00**

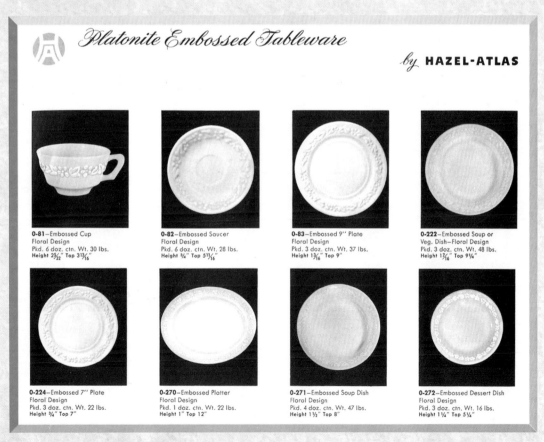

Platonite Embossed Tableware by **HAZEL-ATLAS**

0-81—Embossed Cup
Floral Design
Pkd. 6 doz. ctn. Wt. 30 lbs.
Height 2⁵/₃₂" Top 3¹³/₁₆"

0-82—Embossed Saucer
Floral Design
Pkd. 6 doz. ctn. Wt. 28 lbs.
Height ¾" Top 5¹¹/₁₆"

0-83—Embossed 9" Plate
Floral Design
Pkd. 3 doz. ctn. Wt. 37 lbs.
Height 1³/₁₆" Top 9"

0-222—Embossed Soup or
Veg. Dish—Floral Design
Pkd. 3 doz. ctn. Wt. 48 lbs.
Height 1⁷/₁₆" Top 9¼"

0-224—Embossed 7" Plate
Floral Design
Pkd. 3 doz. ctn. Wt. 22 lbs.
Height ¾" Top 7"

0-270—Embossed Platter
Floral Design
Pkd. 1 doz. ctn. Wt. 22 lbs.
Height 1" Top 12"

0-271—Embossed Soup Dish
Floral Design
Pkd. 4 doz. ctn. Wt. 47 lbs.
Height 1½" Top 8"

0-272—Embossed Dessert Dish
Floral Design
Pkd. 3 doz. ctn. Wt. 16 lbs.
Height 1¼" Top 5¼"

FROM *GLASSWARE BY HAZEL-ATLAS*, 1957 CATALOG, PAGE 30.

"FANCY" – 1929

COLORS - AMETHYST, CRYSTAL, COBALT, GREEN, PLATONITE, PINK

A berry bowl ad from 1929 proclaimed these as fancy "nappies," #732 for large size and #730 for small. The term "nappie" has an Old English origin, meaning a flat-bottomed vessel with sloping sides, either a cup or bowl. Over the years these nappies were produced in amethyst, green, cobalt, crystal, Platonite, and pink. They came both plain rimmed as the original, ruffled, or with scalloped edging. Bowls can also be found with 22K gold trim at rim.

RUFFLED PLATE
Blue, 4½", $15.00.

RUFFLED BOWL – Pink, 8½", $17.50.

DESSERT SET
7-piece, with 22K gold edge,
Cat. #1526/670, **$26.00 – 28.00.**

	CRYSTAL/WHITE	PINK/GREEN	COBALT/AMETHYST
① Bowl, 4¼", beaded edge	$4.00		
② Bowl, 4¼", straight edge	$3.00	$5.00	$10.00
③ Bowl, 4½", ruffled edge	$3.50	$8.00	$15.00
Bowl, 8", beaded rim	$10.00		
Bowl, 8", straight rim	$8.00	$5.00	$20.00
Bowl 8½", ruffled	$10.00	$17.50	$25.00

FLORENTINE NO.1 – HEXAGONAL
COLORS – PINK, GREEN, CRYSTAL, YELLOW, COBALT BLUE

Collectors often confuse Florentine No. 1 and Florentine No. 2 and they need to learn how to distinguish between them. Study the shapes. The jagged edged pieces are hexagonal (six-sided); this edging occurs on all flat pieces of Florentine No. 1. All footed pieces (such as tumblers, shakers, or pitchers) also have that serrated edge on the foot. In Florentine No. 2, all pieces have plain edges. Florentine No. 1 was once promoted as hexagonal and Florentine No. 2 was promoted as round. However, both patterns were advertised and put up for sale in mixed sets. Mingled sets display very well.

The 48-ounce, flat-bottomed pitcher was offered with both Florentine No. 1 and No. 2 sets. It was listed as 54 ounces in catalogs, but usually measures six ounces less. It depends upon the shape of the lip as to how many ounces it will hold before liquid runs out. Flat tumblers with paneled interiors are being found in sets with Florentine No. 1 pitchers. These paneled tumblers should be accepted as Florentine No. 1 rather than Florentine No. 2.

Pink Florentine No. 1 is the most difficult color to find. Pink footed tumblers, covered oval vegetable bowls, and ruffled creamers and sugars are practically unavailable at any price in mint condition.

Fired-on colors have appeared in luncheon sets, but there is little collector zeal for these now. You can find all sorts of colors and colored bands on crystal. One is on the cover.

Florentine No. 1 shakers have been replicated in pink and cobalt blue. Other colors could follow. Some amber is the rarest Florentine color, but only a few items have been discovered. Most sizes of flat tumblers have been found in amber, but no old pitcher.

Both lids to the butter dishes and the oval vegetables are interchangeable in the two Florentine patterns. Candy lids and butter lids are similar in size. The candy lid measures 4¾" in diameter, but the butter dish lid measures 5" exactly. Those measurements are from outside edge to outside edge.

Luncheon set mixtures of red, orange, green, and blue have been seen, with the fired-on colors sprayed over crystal. Orange seems to have been a favorite decorator color in the late 1920s.

PINK

Ashtray, 5½"	$30.00
⑤ Bowl, 5", berry	$18.00
⑨ Bowl, 5", cream soup or ruffled nut	$20.00
Bowl, 6", cereal	$38.00
Bowl, 8½", large berry	$40.00
Bowl, 9½", oval vegtable	$45.00
⑥ Bowl, 9½", oval vegetable and cover	$85.00
Butter dish and cover	$160.00
Butter dish bottom	$85.00
Butter dish top	$75.00
Coaster/ashtray, 3¾"	$30.00
Comport, 3½", ruffled	$18.00
Creamer	$20.00
② Creamer, ruffled	$50.00
Cup	$12.00
Pitcher, 6½", 36 oz., footed	$50.00
Pitcher, 7½", 48 oz., flat, ice lip or none	$225.00
Plate, 6", sherbet	$7.00
Plate, 8½", salad	$12.00
③ Plate, 10", dinner	$30.00
Plate, 10", grill	$22.00
Platter, 11½", oval	$28.00
⑦ Salt and pepper, footed	$55.00
Saucer	$4.00
⑧ Sherbet, 3 oz., footed	$15.00
⑩ Sugar	$12.00
Sugar cover	$30.00
① Sugar, ruffled	$45.00
Tumbler, 3¾", 5 oz., footed, juice	$28.00
Tumbler, 4", 9 oz., ribbed	$22.00
④ Tumbler, 4¾", 10 oz., footed, water	$26.00
Tumbler, 5¼", 12 oz., footed, iced tea	$33.00
Tumbler, 5¼", 9 oz., lemonade (like Floral)	$150.00

FLORENTINE No.1 – HEXAGONAL

GREEN

Ashtray, 5½"	$22.00
Bowl, 5", berry	$14.00
⑨Bowl, 5", cream soup or ruffled nut	$28.00
Bowl, 6", cereal	$25.00
⑯Bowl, 8½", large berry	$30.00
Bowl, 9½", oval vegtable	$35.00
Bowl, 9½", oval vegetable and cover	$55.00
⑮Butter dish and cover	$125.00
Butter dish bottom	$50.00
Butter dish top	$75.00
Coaster/ashtray, 3¾"	$18.00
Comport, 3½", ruffled	$45.00
⑭Creamer	$10.00
②Creamer, ruffled	$50.00
Cup	$8.00
Pitcher, 6½", 36 oz., footed	$40.00
Pitcher, 7½", 48 oz., flat, ice lip or none	$75.00
⑰Plate, 6", sherbet	$6.00
Plate, 8½", salad	$8.00
Plate, 10", dinner	$20.00
⑪Plate, 10", grill	$14.00
Platter, 11½", oval	$20.00
⑦Salt and pepper, footed, pair	$35.00

CRYSTAL 20 – 30% LESS

Saucer	$3.00
⑧Sherbet, 3 oz., footed	$11.00
⑩Sugar	$10.00
Sugar cover	$18.00
Sugar, ruffled	$40.00
⑱Tumbler, 3¼", 4 oz., footed	$16.00
Tumbler, 3¾", 5 oz., footed, juice	$16.00
Tumbler, 4", 9 oz., ribbed	$16.00
Tumbler, 4¾", 10 oz., footed, water	$22.00
Tumbler, 5¼", 12 oz., footed, iced tea	$28.00

COBALT BLUE

Bowl, 5", berry	$25.00
Bowl, 5", cream soup or ruffled nut	$65.00
Comport, 3½", ruffled	$65.00
②Creamer, ruffled	$70.00
Cup	$85.00
Pitcher, 6½", 36 oz., footed	$895.00
Saucer	$17.00
①Sugar, ruffled	$70.00
Tumbler, 3¾", 5 oz. footed, juice	$12.00

CRYSTAL

⑫Bowl, 9½", oval vegtable	$25.00
⑪Plate, 10", dinner	$18.00
⑧Sherbet, 3 oz., footed	$9.00
①Sugar, ruffled	$70.00
⑬Tumbler, 3¾", 5 oz. footed, juice	$4.00

FLORENTINE NO. 1 – HEXAGONAL

YELLOW

⑳ Ashtray, 5½" $30.00	⑭ Creamer $22.00	㉔ Saucer $4.00
⑤ Bowl, 5", berry $18.00	㉓ Cup $12.00	⑧ Sherbet, 3 oz., footed $14.00
Bowl, 6", cereal $32.00	㉒ Pitcher, 6½", 36 oz., footed $45.00	Sugar $12.00
Bowl, 8½", large berry $35.00	Pitcher, 7½", 48 oz., flat,	Sugar cover $30.00
Bowl, 9½", oval vegtable $45.00	ice lip or none $275.00	⑬ Tumbler, 3¾", 5 oz., footed,
Bowl, 9½", oval	⑰ Plate, 6", sherbet $7.00	juice $25.00
vegetable and cover $75.00	㉑ Plate, 8½", salad $12.00	Tumbler, 4¾", 10 oz., footed,
Butter dish and cover $180.00	⑪ Plate, 10", dinner $25.00	water $24.00
Butter dish bottom $85.00	③ Plate, 10", grill $15.00	Tumbler, 5¼", 12 oz.,
Butter dish top $95.00	⑲ Platter, 11½", oval $25.00	footed, iced tea $30.00
Coaster/ashtray, 3¾" $20.00	⑦ Salt and pepper, footed, pair . . .$55.00	

FLORENTINE No.2 – ROUND
COLORS – PINK, GREEN, YELLOW, CRYSTAL, SOME COBALT, AMBER, ICE BLUE

YELLOW

㉗ Bowl, 4½", berry $22.00
⑳ Bowl, 4¾", cream soup $22.00
   Bowl, 5½" $40.00
   Bowl, 6", cereal $40.00
   Bowl, 7½", shallow $100.00
   Bowl, 8", large berry $40.00
   Bowl, 9", oval vegetable
     and cover $95.00
   Butter dish and cover $155.00
   Butter dish bottom $70.00
   Butter dish top $85.00
   Candlesticks, 2¾", pair $70.00
㉛ Candy dish and cover $155.00
   Coaster, 3¼" $22.00
⑮ Coaster/ashtray, 3¾" $30.00
   Coaster/ashtray, 5½" $38.00

⑩ Creamer $12.00
⑥ Cup $10.00
   Custard cup or jello $85.00
㉕ Gravy boat $65.00
   Pitcher, 6¼", 24 oz., cone-ftd . .$165.00
㉓ Pitcher, 7½", 28 oz., cone-ftd . .$35.00
   Pitcher, 7½", 48 oz. $265.00
   Pitcher, 8¼", 76 oz. $450.00
㉘ Plate, 6", sherbet $6.00
   Plate, 6¼", with indent $30.00
㉟ Plate, 8½", salad $10.00
㉚ Plate, 10", dinner $18.00
㉖ Plate, 10¼", grill $18.00
⑭ Platter, 11", oval $25.00
㉔ Platter, 11½", for gravy boat . .$55.00

⑰ Relish dish, 10", 3-part or plain . .$35.00
⑨ Salt and pepper, pair $50.00
⑦ Saucer $4.00
⑤ Sherbet, ftd. $10.00
⑪ Sugar $12.00
⑫ Sugar cover $28.00
㉞ Tray, round, condiment for shakers,
     creamer/sugar $80.00
   Tumbler, 3⅜", 5 oz., juice $22.00
   Tumbler, 4", 9 oz., water $20.00
㉙ Tumbler, 5", 12 oz., tea $55.00
① Tumbler, 3¼", 5 oz., ftd $16.00
② Tumbler, 4", 5 oz., ftd $16.00
③ Tumbler, 5", 9 oz., ftd $35.00
   Vase or parfait, 6" $60.00

FLORENTINE No. 2 – ROUND

GREEN

④ Bowl, 4½", berry $15.00
⑳ Bowl, 4¾", cream soup $18.00
㉒ Bowl, 5", ruffled nut, 2 handled $18.00
Bowl, 5½" $33.00
Bowl, 6", cereal $33.00
Bowl, 8", large berry $30.00
Bowl, 9", oval
    vegetable and cover $65.00
Bowl, 9", flat $27.50
Butter dish and cover $110.00
Butter dish bottom $25.00
Butter dish top $75.00
⑬ Candlesticks, 2¾", pair $50.00
Candy dish and cover $100.00
Coaster, 3¼" $13.00

⑮ Coaster/ashtray, 3¾" $17.50
⑯ Coaster/ashtray, 5½" $20.00
Comport, 3½", ruffled $45.00
⑩ Creamer $9.00
⑥ Cup $9.00
⑧ Custard cup or jello $60.00
㉑ Pitcher, 7½", 48 oz. $75.00
Pitcher, 8¼", 76 oz. $110.00
Plate, 6", sherbet $4.00
㉟ Plate, 8½", salad $8.50
Plate, 10", dinner $16.00
Plate, 10¼", grill $14.00
Plate, 10¼", grill
    with cream soup ring $45.00
⑭ Platter, 11", oval $16.00

⑰ Relish dish, 10", 3-part or plain .$24.00
⑨ Salt and pepper, pair $42.50
⑦ Saucer $3.00
⑤ Sherbet, ftd. $10.00
⑪ Sugar $10.00
⑫ Sugar cover $15.00
Tumbler, 3⅜", 5 oz., juice $14.00
⑲ Tumbler, 3⁹⁄₁₆", 6 oz., blown . . .$18.00
Tumbler, 4", 9 oz., water $16.00
⑱ Tumbler, 5", 12 oz., blown $20.00
Tumbler, 5", 12 oz., tea $35.00
② Tumbler, 3¼", 5 oz., ftd. $15.00
① Tumbler, 4", 5 oz., ftd. $15.00
③ Tumbler, 5", 9 oz., ftd. $35.00
Vase or parfait, 6" $30.00

FLORENTINE No. 2 — ROUND

TUMBLERS
Pink, 4", 9 oz. water, **$20.00.**
*Yellow, 3⅞", 9 oz. water, **$30.00.**
*Note slightly different style.

PINK
③② Bowl, 4½", berry $17.00
②⓪ Bowl, 4¾", cream soup $16.00
Bowl, 8", large berry $32.00
Candy dish and cover $145.00
Coaster, 3¼" $16.00
Comport, 3½", ruffled $45.00
Gravy boat $65.00

AMBER
Cup $50.00
Saucer $15.00
Shercet, ftd. $40.00

Pitcher, 7½", 48 oz. $135.00
Pitcher, 8¼", 76 oz. $225.00
Plate, 8½", salad $8.50
Plate, 10", dinner $15.00
Platter, 11", oval $16.00
Relish dish, 10", 3-part or plain $30.00
③① Tumbler, 3⅜", 5 oz., juice $12.00
④ Tumbler, 4", 9 oz., water $20.00

FIRED COBALT
③⑥ Tumbler, 4", 9 oz., water $15.00

FIRED RED
⑦ Saucer $4.00

CRYSTAL 20 – 30% LESS

FROST —"FROSTED COLOR," "DRIZZLE," "STRING" — 1940S

COLORS – BLACK, TURQUOISE, PINK, WITH WHITE;
PLATONITE WITH BLACK, BLUE, GREEN, RED, ORANGE; AND CRYSTAL WITH GOLD, PINK, ET AL.

Frost decorations were not only popular on Hazel-Atlas wares, but on other company products as well, which leads one to wonder if this treatment was a decorating firm's creation.

COASTER – $5.00.

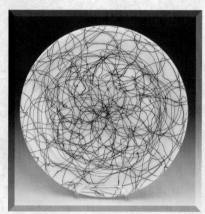

PLATE – 8", $12.00.

WELCH'S REFRESHMENT
WINE, $15.00.

TUMBLER
Turquoise, 5", 12 oz., – **$18.00.**

SHAKER – **$8.00.**

		PLATONITE	BLACK MARBLE, TURQUOISE, ETC.
③	Bowl, 6⅛"	$5.00	$10.00
②	Bowl, 10½"	$12.00	$20.00
	Coaster	$5.00	
①	Creamer	$8.00	$12.00
④	Cup	$6.00	$8.00
	Plate, 8"	$12.00	$20.00
⑤	Saucer	$2.00	$3.00
	Shaker, pair	$15.00	$25.00
	Sugar	$8.00	$12.00
	Tumbler	$10.00	$15.00
⑥	Utensils, plastic salad, pair	$8.00	$10.00

GOTHIC – "BIG TOP"

COLORS – CRYSTAL AND MILK GLASS

A Lexington, Kentucky, company manufactured Big Top peanut butter and used this glassware to distribute its product. Known pieces in this pattern include cup, saucer, 8" luncheon plate, 8-oz. sherbet, 10-oz. tumbler, and 7 oz. goblet. The 7-oz. juice tumbler is the item most collectors are missing; evidently avid peanut butter fans didn't buy the smaller size.

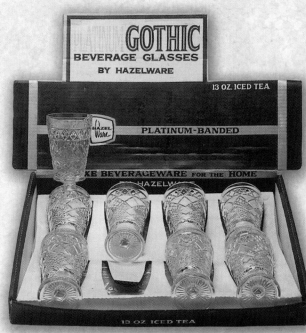

TUMBLER
Platonite, 10 oz., **$3.00**.

CRYSTAL	
④ Cup..	$6.00
③ Plate, 8", luncheon	$8.00
⑤ Saucer....................................	$3.00
① Sherbet, 8 oz.	$3.00
② Tumbler, 7 oz. juice or parfait	$18.00
⑥ Tumbler, 10 oz............................	$5.00

Get this exclusive "Early American" Glassware every time you buy BIG TOP Peanut Butter

LOOK! New glamour for your table!

Look! Lovely matching sherbet glass or dessert dish. Start building a set of this beautiful stemware now.

Look! Isn't this water goblet a beauty! Exclusive "Early American" design in large dinner size.

The PEANUT BUTTER with the fresh-roasted flavor of peanuts at the circus!

Big Top's Roto-roasting—that's the secret that brings out *all* the golden goodness of the peanuts . . . gives Big Top Peanut Butter its delicious fresh-roasted flavor. Whip-blending makes it so creamy, too, for easy spreading. Yes, Big Top really tastes as tempting as it looks in these lovely crystal-clear goblets and sherbets. Treat your family to Big Top and start collecting this "Early American" stemware to sparkle on *your* table!

Also comes in handy Refrigerator Jars

Big Top is another great food product from Procter & Gamble

BIG TOP PEANUT BUTTER

Copr. W. T. Young Foods, Inc., subsidiary of The Procter & Gamble Company

AT YOUR STORE NOW, OR COMING SOON!

1960s Big Top Peanut Butter advertisement.

IVY - 1950s

The Ivy lamp is made from tumblers, a bowl, and a connector, and was doubtless put together by some company other than Hazel-Atlas. We found a lamp after we'd photographed this one with the original tan paper shade having a dark green Ivy border at the bottom. See various other Ivy patterned products on the cover and throughout the book, i.e. various forms of bowls, shakers and mugs. Ivy was a popular design in the 50s as all sorts of products can be found with this decoration — including linens.

IVY LAMP
Made from tumblers, bowl and connector. 13¼", **$30.00.**

KITCHEN CHEF - 1950s

Plates in this pattern are found on Federal's and Anchor Hocking's Fire-King blanks. Two kinds of shakers are found: one on Bartlett-Collins blank and one on Anchor Hocking's blanks. We've found the mugs to be Hazel-Atlas products. This suggests that some decorating company is responsible for this pattern, and/or it was a premium product made specifically for some company as a promotional item.

PLATE
Federal, **$10.00.**

MUG
Hazel-Atlas, **$12.00.**

SHAKERS – 3¾"
Salt, **$30.00.**
Pepper, **$30.00.**
Salt & pepper, **$65.00.**

Mug (Hazel-Atlas)	$12.00
Plate (Fire-King)	$12.50
Plate (Federal)	$10.00
Shaker, pair (Bartlett-Collins)	$65.00
Shaker, pair (Fire-King)	$125.00

"KITCHEN UTENSILS" – "KITCHEN AIDS" – 1950s

COLORS – PLATONITE WITH RED, ORANGE, TURQUOISE, BROWN

Since Anchor Hocking bowls are known with a Kitchen Aids design also, you need to specify you want the Hazel-Atlas ones if you use that terminology for this design.

MIXING BOWLS
5", cereal, $12.00.
6", $15.00.
7", $20.00.
8", $25.00.
MUG – $12.00.

Bowl, 5" cereal	$12.00
Bowl, 6" mixing	$15.00
③ Bowl, 7" mixing	$20.00
⑥ Bowl, 8" mixing	$25.00
① Cup	$6.00
⑤ Mug	$12.00
Plate, 7"	$7.50
④ Plate, 8⅞", dinner	$10.00
② Saucer, 5⅝"	$2.00

MIXING BOWL
8", $25.00.

MODERNISTIC
COLONIAL BLOCK*

COLORS – GREEN, CRYSTAL, BLACK, PINK, AND RARE IN COBALT BLUE; WHITE IN 1950s

Colonial Block is most often found in green and consequently, most collectors buy it rather than pink. Original ads called Colonial Block a modernistic design and "modernism" was the dernier cri (latest fashion) of the time. You will find an occasional crystal piece or white creamer and sugar sets. A few black and frosted green Colonial Block powder jars are being found.

BOWLS – 7", **$12.00**; 4¼", **$4.00**; 4¼", **$4.00**.

PITCHER
Cat. #13025, 44 oz., **$25.00**.

COLONIAL COVERED DISHES
8- sided knobs, 6¾", marked HA, **$25.00 – 30.00 each.**

CREAMERS
Cobalt Blue, **$300.00 – 325.00**.
Platonite, **$5.00**.
SUGAR – **$8.00**.
With lid, **$15.00**.

*SEE PAGE 172 FOR COLONIAL BLOCK ADVERTISEMENT.

MODERNISTIC
COLONIAL BLOCK*

CRYSTAL
② Bowl, 4¼" $4.00
① Bowl, 7" $12.00
⑤ Butter dish, 6¾" $30.00
   Butter dish bottom $5.00
   Butter dish top $25.00
⑨ Butter tub, 4¾" $25.00
⑩ Candy jar with cover $25.00
⑥ Creamer $6.00
   Goblet $6.00
   Pitcher $35.00
   Powder jar with lid $12.00
③ Sherbet $4.00
⑧ Sugar $7.00
⑦ Sugar lid $8.00
④ Tumbler, 5¼", 5 oz., footed $25.00

WHITE
   Bowl, 5⅜", cereal $5.00
   Bowl, 4½", utility, 2⅜" deep $15.00
   Creamer $5.00
   Sugar $8.00
   Sugar lid $7.00

GREEN OR PINK
② Bowl, 4¼" $11.00
① Bowl, 7" $25.00
⑤ Butter dish, 6¾" $45.00
   Butter dish bottom $12.50
⑨ Butter dish top $32.50
   Butter tub, 4¾" $45.00
⑩ Candy jar with cover $42.00
⑥ Creamer $12.00
   Goblet $15.00
   Pitcher $50.00
   Powder jar with lid $17.50
③ Sherbet $8.00
⑧ Sugar $10.00
⑦ Sugar lid $15.00
④ Tumbler, 5¼", 5 oz., footed $75.00

COBALT
⑥ Creamer $300.00

*SEE PAGE 172 FOR COLONIAL BLOCK ADVERTISEMENT.

TABLE GLASSWARE

MATCHED TABLEWARE

GREEN . . . Colonial Block
Pattern . . . Heavy Pressed.

4 In. Creamers
50R-3610—3 doz in carton, 30 lbs. **Doz** .84

6 In. Sugar Bowls
50R-3612—3 doz in carton, 48 lbs. **Doz** .92

4¾ In. Butter Dishes
May be used for jelly or preserves.
50R-3611—3 doz in carton, 38 lbs. **Doz** .85

6¾ In. Butter Dishes
50R-3613—3 doz in carton, 62 lbs. **Doz** .92

BERRY BOWLS—NAPPIES

POPULAR DESIGNS . . . pressed glass . . . deep shapes.

GREEN—Block Design—Star Bottoms

7 In. Berry Bowls
50R-3920—3 doz in carton, 50 lbs. **Doz** .89

4½ In. Nappies
50R-3900—6 doz in carton, 35 lbs. **Doz** .38

GREEN—Process Etched "Florentine" design

8 In. Berry Bowls
50R-3921—2 doz in carton, 32 lbs. **Doz** .95

4½ In. Nappies
50R-3911—6 doz in carton, 28 lbs. **Doz** .39

8½ In. Berry Bowls
"Sierra" panel design, extra deep shape, 4 doz in carton, 60 lbs
50R-3924—Green
50R-3925—Rose-pink **Doz** .92

8 In. Berry Bowls
"Adam" design, process etched floral design, fluted pattern, 4 doz in carton, 62 lbs
50R-3926—Green
50R-3927—Rose-pink **Doz** 1.05

4 In. Nappies
Process-etched clover leaf border, 6 doz in carton, 26 lbs.
50R-1096—Green . . . . . **Doz** .25

SYRUP PITCHERS

Green
12 oz., 6¼ in., blown, removable metal top.
50R-3550—2 doz in carton, 26 lbs. **Doz** 1.25

Crystal
9½ oz., 4⅜ in., pressed, optic fluted, removable metal top.
50R-3551—2 doz in carton, 20 lbs. **Doz** 1.35

Crystal
15 oz., 5⅝ in., pressed prism fluted, removable metal top.
50R-3560—1 doz in carton, 17 lbs. **Doz** 2.15

VINEGAR OR OIL BOTTLES

Crystal
8 oz., 6 in., pressed.
50R-3570—2 doz in carton, 20 lbs. **Doz** .80

Crystal
6 oz., 5¾ in., thin blown.
50R-3572—2 doz in carton, 15 lbs. **Doz** .89

Asstd. Crystal & Green
5 oz., 6¼ in., pot glass.
50R-3590—1 doz in carton, 12 lbs. **Doz** 2.15

CEREAL DISHES

5 in., extra deep, light pressed, process-etched clover leaf border. 4 doz in carton, 25 lbs.

50R-1037—Topaz . . . . . **Doz** .39

SALAD PLATES

Green
8 in., pressed, process etched clover leaf border.
50R-1091—3 doz in carton, 33 lbs . . . . **Doz** .60

CAKE PLATES

Green
10¼ in., pressed, dewdrop design, embossed floral and leaf border.
50R-3985—1 doz in carton, 25 lbs . . . . . **Doz** 2.25

SUGARS, CREAMERS AND SETS

3¾ in., pressed, process-etched clover leaf border, 3 doz in carton, 17 lbs.

SUGARS—
50R-1094—Green . . . . **Doz** .36

CREAMERS—
50R-1093—Green . . . . **Doz** .36

Sugar & Creamer Sets
Sugar and creamer 3½ in., pressed.
50R-3670—2 doz sets in carton, 24 lbs . . . . **Doz sets** 80c

SALT & PEPPER SHAKERS

Crystal
3¼ in., concave panels, metal top.
50R-3500—3 doz in box, 7 lbs. **Doz** .36

Green
3 in., modernistic design, aluminum top.
50R-3504—3 doz in carton, 10 lbs. **Doz** .42

Green
3¾ in., chromium plated top.
50R-3506—4 doz in carton, 15 lbs. **Doz** .45

Crystal
4¼ in. nickeled top.
50R-3531—2 doz in case, 10 lbs. **Doz** .79

MISCELLANEOUS ITEMS

Tooth Pick Holders
2¼ x 2¼ in., thin blown crystal, genuine cut.
50-3730—1 doz in box . . . . **Doz** .78

Opal Glass Mugs
3½ in., heavy opal glass.
50R-3733—3 doz in carton, 40 lbs. **Doz** .85

Egg Cups
4½ in., double deck, heavy pressed crystal.
50R-3732—2 doz in carton, 18 lbs. **Doz** .87

Milk Pitchers
20 oz., 5 in., green, pressed.
50R-3673—2 doz in carton, 30 lbs. **Doz** .92

GREEN 7-PC. BERRY SETS

8 in. bowl, 6 nappies 4¼ in., pressed, deep shape, imitation cut.
50R-3990—½ doz sets in carton, 25 lbs . . . . **Doz sets** 3.95

BUTLER BROTHERS

FROM BUTLER BROTHERS CATALOG, C. 1927.

MODERNTONE

COLORS – AMETHYST, COBALT BLUE; SOME CRYSTAL, PINK, AND PLATONITE FIRED-ON COLORS

Moderntone is popular for its rich coloring and for its uncomplicated style. It is more reasonably priced today than many of its counterpart patterns made in cobalt blue or amethyst. It originally cost about the same as those other patterns.

The cheese dish remains the highest priced piece of Moderntone. This cheese dish is fundamentally a salad plate with a metal cover and wooden cutting board inside the lid.

PLATE
Cobalt with trim, 6¾", $12.00.
JOKE PLATE
Platonite, 5⅞", $10.00.
PLATE
Crystal, 6¾", $6.00.

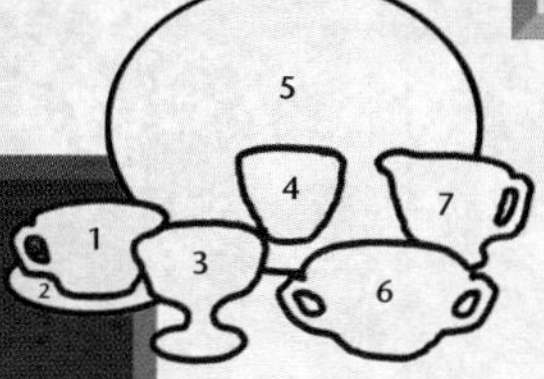

AMETHYST

⑥ Bowl, 4¾", cream soup	. . . . .	$20.00
Bowl, 5", berry	. . . .	$25.00
Bowl, 5", cream soup, ruffled	. .	$33.00
Bowl, 6½", cereal	. . . .	$75.00
Bowl, 7½", soup	. . . .	$100.00
Bowl, 8¾", large berry	. . . . . .	$40.00
⑦ Creamer	. . . .	$11.00
① Cup	. . . .	$12.00
④ Cup (handle-less) or custard	.	$15.00
Plate, 5⅞", sherbet	. . . .	$5.00
Plate, 6¾", salad	. . . .	$10.00
Plate, 7¾", luncheon	. . . .	$10.00
Plate, 8⅞", dinner	. . . .	$13.00
Plate, 10½", sandwich	. . . . . .	$40.00
Platter, 11", oval	. . . .	$37.50
⑤ Platter, 12", oval	. . . .	$45.00
Salt and pepper, pair	. . . .	$40.00
② Saucer	. . . .	$3.00
③ Sherbet	. . . .	$12.00
Sugar	. . . .	$12.00
Sugar lid (metal)	. . . .	$37.00
Tumbler, 5 oz.	. . . .	$40.00
Tumbler, 9 oz.	. . . .	$30.00
Tumbler, 12 oz.	. . . .	$90.00

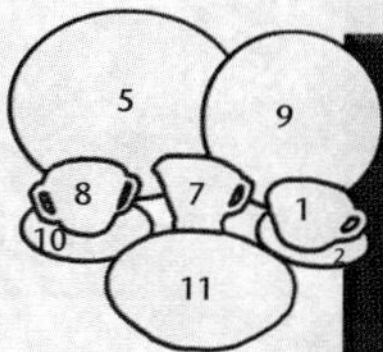

CRYSTAL

⑪ Bowl, 7½", soup	. . . .	$25.00
⑦ Creamer	. . . .	$8.00
① Cup	. . . .	$5.00
⑩ Plate, 5⅞", sherbet	. . . .	$4.00
Plate, 6¾", salad	. . . .	$10.00
Plate, 7¾", luncheon	. . . .	$18.00
⑨ Plate, 8⅞", dinner	. . . .	$10.00
Plate, 10½", sandwich	. . . . . .	$20.00
Platter, 11", oval	. . . .	$25.00
⑤ Platter, 12", oval	. . . .	$45.00
② Saucer	. . . .	$2.00
⑧ Sugar	. . . .	$8.00
Whiskey 1½ oz.	. . . .	$15.00

MODERNTONE

RITZ BLUE DISH SET

Creamer, $12.50   Cup, $12.00
Sugar, $13.00   Saucer, $4.00
BOXED SET, $200.00

RITZ BLUE

Ashtray, 7¾", match holder in center $20.00	⑱ Plate, 7¾", luncheon $10.00
⑥ Bowl, 4¾", cream soup $20.00	⑨ Plate, 8⅞", dinner $13.00
⑭ Bowl, 5", berry $25.00	⑰ Plate, 10½", sandwich $40.00
⑯ Bowl, 5", cream soup, ruffled $33.00	⑫ Platter, 11", oval $37.50
⑮ Bowl, 6½", cereal $75.00	⑤ Platter, 12", oval $45.00
⑪ Bowl, 7½", soup $100.00	Salt and pepper, pair $40.00
⑬ Bowl, 8¾", large berry $40.00	② Saucer $4.00
⑳ Butter dish, with metal cover $40.00	③ Sherbet $12.00
㉑ Cheese dish, 7", with metal cover $40.00	⑧ Sugar $13.00
⑦ Creamer $12.50	⑲ Sugar lid (metal) $37.50
① Cup $12.00	㉓ Tumbler, 5 oz. $40.00
④ Cup (handle-less) or custard $15.00	㉔ Tumbler, 9 oz. $30.00
㉕ Cup (handle-less) or mustard with lid $18.00	Tumbler, 12 oz. $90.00
Plate, 5⅞", sherbet $5.00	㉒ Whiskey, 1½ oz. $45.00
㉘ Plate, 6¾", salad $10.00	

MODERNTONE

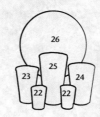

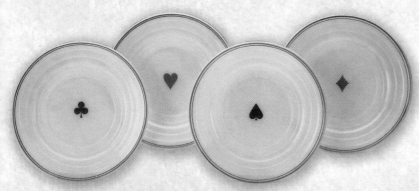

BRIDGE SET PLATES
Club, heart, spade, diamond, 7¾" – **$18.00 each.**

PLATONITE
Sherbet, $2.50.
Sugar, $4.00.
Salt and pepper, $13.00 pair.
Tumbler, 9 oz., $6.00.

PLATONITE WITH HAIRLINE & STRIPE
Sherbet, $8.00.

PLATONITE WITH STRIPE
Footed custard, $6.00.

PLATONITE WITH STRIPE
Cream soup bowl, 4¾", $10.00.
Berry bowl with rim, 5", $7.00.
Salt and pepper, $14.00 pair.
Sherbet, $8.00.

MODERNTONE

PLATONITE WITH HAIRLINE & STRIPE
Footed custard, **$6.00.**
Sherbet plate, 6¾", **$5.00.**
Cone footed tumbler, **$9.00.**

BLUE WILLOW
Sandwich plate, 10½", **$40.00.**
Cup, **$25.00.**
Oval platter, 12", **$50.00.**

DECO BLUE OR RED WILLOW
⑥ Bowl, 4¾", cream soup $25.00
⑤ Bowl, 5", berry, with rim . . .$17.50
Bowl, 8", with rim $45.00
Bowl, 8¾", large berry $45.00
⑧ Creamer $25.00
⑯ Cup $25.00
Plate, 6¾", sherbet $11.00
⑪ Plate, 8⅞", dinner $40.00
⑬ Plate, 10", sandwich $40.00
Platter, 11", oval $40.00
⑨ Platter, 12", oval $50.00
⑰ Saucer $5.00
② Sherbet $22.00
① Sugar $25.00

MODERNTONE

PLATONITE WITH STRIPES
Sherbet, **$8.00.**
Luncheon plate, 7¾", **$7.00.**
Cup, **$8.00.**
Berry bowl with rim, 5", **$7.00.**

PLATONITE WITH STRIPES

Item	Price	Item	Price
Bowl, 4¾", cream soup	$10.00	⑪ Plate, 7¾", luncheon	$7.00
⑭ Bowl, 7½", soup	$25.00	⑫ Plate, 8⅞", dinner	$12.00
⑤ Bowl, 5", berry, with rim	$7.00	⑬ Plate, 10½", sandwich	$22.00
⑮ Bowl, 8", with rim	$22.00	⑨ Platter, 12", oval	$25.00
⑧ Creamer	$12.50	③ Salt and pepper, pair	$18.00
⑯ Cup	$8.00	⑰ Saucer	$3.00
Custard, ftd.	$9.00	② Sherbet	$8.00
⑱ Mug, 4", 8 oz.	$12.00	① Sugar	$12.50
⑩ Plate, 5⅞", sherbet	$5.00		

MODERNTONE
FIRED-ON COLORS

YELLOW

PINK

BLUE

GREEN

PASTEL COLORS

	Bowl, 4¾", cream soup		$6.50
⑤	Bowl, 5", berry, with rim		$5.00
㉑	Bowl, 5", berry, without rim		$6.00
	Bowl, 5", deep cereal, with white		$7.50
⑳	Bowl, 5", deep cereal, without white		$10.00
	Bowl, 8", with rim		$15.00
	Bowl, 8", without rim		$22.00
⑧	Creamer		$4.00
⑯	Cup		$3.50
	Plate, 6¾", sherbet		$4.00
⑫	Plate, 7¾", luncheon		$5.00
⑪	Plate, 8⅞", dinner		$6.00
⑬	Plate, 10½", sandwich		$15.00
	Platter, 12", oval		$15.00
③	Salt and pepper, pair.		$16.00
⑰	Saucer		$1.00
②	Sherbet		$4.50
①	Sugar		$4.00
④	Tumbler, 9 oz.		$9.00

MODERNTONE
FIRED-ON COLORS

CHARTREUSE
Sherbet, $9.00.
Saucer, $5.00.
Cup, $8.00.
Dinner plate, 8⅞", $13.00.

GRAY
Berry bowl without rim, 5", $12.00.
Sandwich plate, 10½", $25.00.
Cup, $8.00.
Saucer, $5.00.

ORANGE
Creamer, $8.00.
Cream soup bowl, 4¾", $11.00.
Tumbler, 9 oz., $10.00.
Bowl with rim, 8", $30.00.
Berry bowl with rim, 5", $12.00.

GOLD
Deep cereal bowl, without white, $15.00.
Oval platter, 12" $32.00.
Sherbet, $9.00.
Berry bowl without rim, 5", $12.00.

MODERNTONE
FIRED-ON COLORS

TURQUOISE

GREEN

COBALT

BURGUNDY

COBALT, TURQUOISE, ORANGE	
⑧ Bowl, 4¾", cream soup	$11.00
⑪ Bowl, 5", berry, with rim	$12.00
③ Bowl, 5", berry, without rim	$8.00
Bowl, 5", deep cereal, with white	$12.00
Bowl, 8", with rim	$30.00
Bowl, 8", without rim	$30.00
Creamer	$8.00
⑤ Cup	$7.00
Plate, 6¾", sherbet	$6.00
⑮ Plate, 7¾", luncheon	$8.00
⑰ Plate, 8⅞", dinner	$12.00
⑬ Plate, 10½", sandwich	$12.00
Platter, 12", oval	$22.00
⑭ Salt and pepper, pair.	$20.00
⑥ Saucer	$4.00
② Sherbet	$7.00
Sugar	$8.00
⑨ Tumbler, 9 oz.	$10.00

BURGUNDY, CHARTREUSE, GRAY, RUST, GOLD	
③ Bowl, 5", berry, without rim	$12.00
① Bowl, 5", deep cereal, without white	$15.00
⑯ Bowl, 8", without rim	$40.00
⑦ Creamer	$11.00
⑤ Cup	$8.00
Plate, 6¾", sherbet	$8.00
⑰ Plate, 8⅞", dinner	$13.00
⑬ Plate, 10½", sandwich	$25.00
Platter, 12", oval	$22.00
Salt and pepper, pair.	$20.00
⑥ Saucer	$5.00
Sherbet	$9.00
⑫ Sugar	$11.00
⑨ Tumbler, 9 oz.	$30.00

MODERNTONE
CHILDREN'S SETS

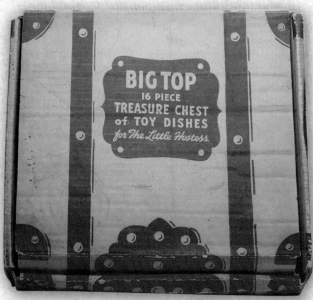

BIG TOP PEANUT BUTTER DISH SET
  Two views
  Without box, **$200.00.**
  With advertising box, **$250.00.**

FRONT OF DEEP BOX

SEE PAGE 184 FOR BACK OF BOX.

MODERNTONE
CHILDREN'S SETS

LITTLE HOSTESS WHITE PARTY SET
Without box, $395.00.
With box, $425.00.

LITTLE HOSTESS PINK & BLACK PARTY SET
Without box, $360.00.
With box, $395.00.

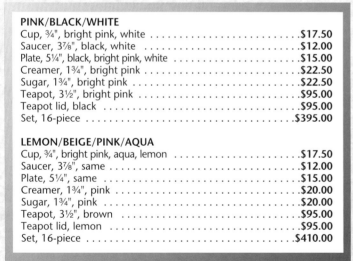

PINK/BLACK/WHITE
Cup, ¾", bright pink, white $17.50
Saucer, 3⅞", black, white $12.00
Plate, 5¼", black, bright pink, white $15.00
Creamer, 1¾", bright pink $22.50
Sugar, 1¾", bright pink $22.50
Teapot, 3½", bright pink $95.00
Teapot lid, black $95.00
Set, 16-piece $395.00

LEMON/BEIGE/PINK/AQUA
Cup, ¾", bright pink, aqua, lemon $17.50
Saucer, 3⅞", same $12.00
Plate, 5¼", same $15.00
Creamer, 1¾", pink $20.00
Sugar, 1¾", pink $20.00
Teapot, 3½", brown $95.00
Teapot lid, lemon $95.00
Set, 16-piece $410.00

LITTLE HOSTESS LEMON/BEIGE PARTY SET
Without box, $375.00.
With box, $410.00.

MODERNTONE
CHILDREN'S SETS

LITTLE HOSTESS PARTY SET
Without box, **$200.00.**
With box, **$235.00.**

LITTLE HOSTESS BURGUNDY PARTY SET
Without box, **$195.00.**
With box, **$230.00.**

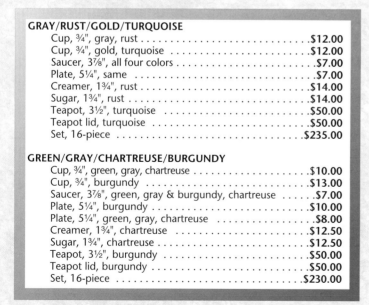

GRAY/RUST/GOLD/TURQUOISE
Cup, ¾", gray, rust $12.00
Cup, ¾", gold, turquoise $12.00
Saucer, 3⅞", all four colors $7.00
Plate, 5¼", same $7.00
Creamer, 1¾", rust $14.00
Sugar, 1¾", rust $14.00
Teapot, 3½", turquoise $50.00
Teapot lid, turquoise $50.00
Set, 16-piece $235.00

GREEN/GRAY/CHARTREUSE/BURGUNDY
Cup, ¾", green, gray, chartreuse $10.00
Cup, ¾", burgundy $13.00
Saucer, 3⅞", green, gray & burgundy, chartreuse $7.00
Plate, 5¼", burgundy $10.00
Plate, 5¼", green, gray, chartreuse $8.00
Creamer, 1¾", chartreuse $12.50
Sugar, 1¾", chartreuse $12.50
Teapot, 3½", burgundy $50.00
Teapot lid, burgundy $50.00
Set, 16-piece $230.00

LITTLE HOSTESS PARTY SET, BOX ONLY
Excellent condition, **$30.00 – 35.00.**

MODERNTONE
CHILDREN'S SETS

LITTLE HOSTESS PASTEL PARTY SET
14 piece without teapot
Without box, **$100.00.**
With box, **$135.00.**

BACK OF DEEP BOX

LITTLE HOSTESS PASTEL PARTY SET
14 piece without teapot
Without black box, **$100.00.**
With black box, **$135.00.**

LITTLE HOSTESS PASTEL PARTY SET
14 piece without teapot
Without green box, **$100.00.**
With green box, **$135.00.**

PASTEL/PINK/GREEN/BLUE/YELLOW

Cup, ¾", all four colors	$8.00
Saucer, 3⅞", same	$6.00
Plate, 5¼", same	$9.00
Creamer, 1¾", pink	$15.00
Sugar, 1¾", pink	$15.00
Set, 14-piece	$100.00

MOROCCAN AMETHYST
COLOR – AMETHYST

Just as colors of today will define our era, this rich, purple color could be identified with the 1960s. Hazel-Atlas called all their wares in this delightful shade of purple Moroccan Amethyst, and these goods have found a loyal following with collectors. As with Capri, various designs have acquired names based upon shapes. Square or rectangular based pieces are being called Colony as they are in Capri. Moroccan also has a Swirl just as in Capri. There are octagonal and pentagonal shape names which are self explanatory.

Pieces of Moroccan Amethyst that are beginning to disappear from markets include the ice bucket, 8 oz., old-fashioned tumbler, cocktail shaker, and the short, covered candy dish. The lids to the candy jars are interchangeable.

OCTAGONAL
- 33 Bowl, 4¾", fruit $8.00
- 9 Cup $5.00
- 8 Plate, 5¾" $4.50
- 12 Plate, 9¾", dinner $4.50
- 11 Plate, 8" $12.00
- 10 Saucer $1.50

PUNCH SET
$60.00 – 65.00.

VASE
Ruffled, with decal, 8½", $40.00.

MOROCCAN AMETHYST

COLONY SQUARE

Ashtray, 8", square $13.00	⑭ Plate, 8", snack with indent $10.00
⑥ Bowl, 5¾", square, deep $10.00	④ Plate, 12", round $15.00
① Bowl, 6", round $12.00	㉜ Plate, 12", sandwich, with metal handle $17.50
⑤ Bowl, 7¾", oval $16.00	⑩ Saucer $1.50
② Bowl, 9¾", rectangular $14.00	⑰ Tumbler, 4 oz., juice, 2¾" $8.50
⑦ Bowl, 9¾", rectangular, with metal handle . . .$18.00	⑬ Tumbler, 8 oz., old fashioned, 3¼" $8.00
③ Bowl, 10¾" $30.00	⑯ Tumbler, 9 oz., water, 4¼" $8.00
⑨ Cup $5.00	⑮ Tumbler, 12 oz., iced tea, 5" $10.00
⑫ Plate, 8" $12.00	

MOROCCAN AMETHYST

SWIRL

③① Candy with lid, short	....	$38.00
②⑦ Candy bottom with base, top of chip and dip set	....	$20.00
②⑨ Candy with lid, tall	....	$38.00
Chip and dip, 10¾" & 5¾" bowls in metal holder	....	$40.00
②⑥ Coaster, platonite**	....	$4.00
①⑧ Cocktail with stirrer, 6¼", 16 oz., with lip		$32.00
②③ Cocktail shaker with lid	....	$30.00
Cup	....	$5.00

②⑧ Ice bucket, 6"	....	$38.00
③⓪ Salt shaker, pair	....	$95.00
Saucer	....	$1.50
②② Tumbler, 4 oz., 2½", cocktail	....	$8.50
②① Tumbler, 5 oz., 3½", juice	....	$6.00
①③ Tumbler, 8 oz., old fashioned, 3¼"	...	$8.00
②⑤ Tumbler, 11 oz., water, 4⅝"	....	$10.00
①⑨ Tumbler, 16 oz., iced tea, 6½"	......	$15.00
②④ Vase, 8½", ruffled	....	$35.00
		** packed with iced teas.

ALSO AVAILABLE IN MOROCCAN AMETHYST

Ashtray, 3¼", triangular	$5.50
Ashtray, 3¼", round	$5.50
Ashtray, 6⅞", triangular	$9.50
Candle, star shape, 4½"	$35.00
Candy, open with metal, top of chip and dip set	$20.00
Goblet, 4½ oz., 4", wine, crinkled bottom	$10.00
Goblet, 7½ oz., 4¼", sherbet, crinkled bottom	$8.00
Goblet, 5½ oz., 4⅜", juice, crinkled bottom	$9.00
Goblet, 9 oz., 5½", water, crinkled bottom	$10.00
Plate, 7¼", salad	$7.00
Plate, 10", fan shaped, snack with cup rest	$7.00
Tumbler, 4 oz., juice, 2¾", crinkled bottom	$7.00
Tumbler, 9 oz., water, 4¼", crinkled bottom	$8.00
Tumbler, 11 oz., water, 4¼", crinkled bottom	$10.00

NEW CENTURY

COLORS – GREEN; SOME CRYSTAL AND WITH TRIMS, PINK, AMETHYST, AND COBALT

New Century is a Hazel-Atlas pattern that has attracted collectors for years. Green is the chosen color since sets can only be amassed in that color. A few pieces are found in crystal, but not enough to assemble a set, according to some that tried to do so. Crystal prices are on par with green, even with little demand.

Thirty years into collecting Depression glass, New Century bowls are all but impossible to find. Pink, cobalt blue, and amethyst New Century have only been encountered in water sets and an occasional cup or saucer. Only flat tumblers have been found in these colors.

AMETHYST TUMBLERS
5", 10 oz., **$22.00.**
5¼", 12 oz., **$30.00.**
4¼", 8 oz., **$20.00.**
3½", 5 oz., **$12.00.**

PINK
Plate, salad, 8½", **$14.00.**
Tumbler, 9 oz., 4¼", **$20.00.**
Pitcher, 7¾", 60 oz., without ice lip, **$35.00.**

CUP
Crystal, with trim, **$10.00.**

CRYSTAL
Powder jar, **$25.00.**
Ashtray/coaster, 5⅜", **$30.00.**
Whiskey, 2½", 1½ oz., **$22.00.**
COBALT
Tumbler, 5", 10 oz., **$22.00.**
Tumbler, 4¼", 9 oz., **$20.00.**
Pitcher, 8", 80 oz., with ice lip, **$42.00.**

NEW CENTURY

GREEN OR CRYSTAL

⑨ Ashtray/coaster, 5⅜" $30.00
⑤ Bowl, 4½", berry $30.00
② Bowl, 4¾", cream soup $22.00
① Bowl, 8", large berry $28.00
④ Bowl, 9", covered casserole $95.00
Butter dish and cover $65.00
⑦ Cup $10.00
⑭ Creamer $15.00
⑲ Decanter and stopper $75.00
Goblet, 2½ oz., wine $33.00
⑪ Goblet, 3¼ oz., cocktail $33.00
Pitcher, 7¾", 60 oz.,
with or without ice lip $35.00

Pitcher, 8", 80 oz.
with or without ice lip $40.00
Plate, 6", sherbet $8.00
⑥ Plate, 7⅛", breakfast $10.00
Plate, 8½", salad $14.00
③ Plate, 10", dinner $18.00
⑮ Plate, 10", grill $20.00
⑯ Platter, 11", oval $25.00
Powder jar $25.00
⑳ Salt and pepper, pair $40.00
⑧ Saucer $3.00
⑩ Sherbet, 3" $12.00
⑫ Sugar $10.00

⑬ Sugar lid $18.00
Tumbler, 3½", 5 oz. $18.00
Tumbler, 3½", 8 oz. $28.00
⑱ Tumbler, 4¼", 9 oz. $22.00
Tumbler, 5", 10 oz. $22.00
㉑ Tumbler, 5¼", 12 oz. $33.00
Tumbler, 4", 5 oz., ftd. $22.00
⑰ Tumbler, 4⅞", 9 oz., ftd. $25.00
Whiskey, 2½", 1½ oz. $22.00

AMETHYST, COBALT OR PINK

Cup $20.00
Pitcher, 7¾", 60 oz., with or without ice lip $35.00
Pitcher, 8", 80 oz., with or without ice lip $42.00
Saucer $7.50
Tumbler, 3½", 5 oz. $12.00
Tumbler, 4¼", 9 oz. $20.00
Tumbler, 5", 10 oz. $22.00
Tumbler, 5¼", 12 oz. $30.00

NEWPORT

COLORS – COBALT BLUE, AMETHYST; SOME PINK, PLATONITE WHITE, AND FIRED-ON COLORS

Collectors favor cobalt blue in this pattern. Not much pink Newport is found today. Platonite Newport was made mostly during the 1950s. Newport and Moderntone are among the few Depression ware sets you can assemble in amethyst.

COBALT
	Bowl, 4¾", berry	$20.00
	Bowl, 4¾", cream soup	$25.00
	Bowl, 5¼", cereal	$40.00
	Bowl, 8¼", large berry	$45.00
③	Cup	$14.00
⑮	Creamer	$16.00
	Plate, 5⅞", sherbet	$8.00
⑤	Plate, 8½", luncheon	$15.00
	Plate, 8¹³⁄₁₆", dinner	$22.00
	Plate, 11¾", sandwich	$45.00
	Platter, 11¾", oval	$50.00
②	Salt and pepper, pair	$50.00
④	Saucer	$5.00
	Sherbet	$15.00
	Sugar	$16.00
①	Tumbler, 4½", 9 oz	$45.00

AMETHYST
⑨	Bowl, 4¾", berry	$17.00
⑭	Bowl, 4¾", cream soup	$24.00
	Bowl, 5¼", cereal	$35.00
	Bowl, 8¼", large berry	$45.00
	Cup	$12.00
	Creamer	$12.00
⑫	Plate, 5⅞", sherbet	$ 8.00
⑪	Plate, 8½", luncheon	$16.00
	Plate, 11¾", sandwich	$40.00
⑬	Platter, 11¾", oval	$43.00
	Salt and pepper, pair	$40.00
	Saucer	$ 5.00
	Sherbet	$15.00
⑩	Sugar	$16.00
	Tumbler, 4½", 9 oz	$40.00

PINK
Berry bowl, large, 8¼", **$20.00**.
Berry bowl, 4¾", **$8.00**.
Sherbet, **$10.00**.

NEWPORT

FIRED-ON COLORS

	Bowl, 4¾", berry	$7.50
	Bowl, 4¾", cream soup	$8.00
	Bowl, 8¼, large berry	$14.00
	Cake set with metal handle & server	$55.00
⑦	Cup	$6.00
	Creamer	$7.50
	Plate, 6", sherbet	$1.50
⑤	Plate, 8½", luncheon	$5.00
③	Plate, 11½", sandwich	$14.00
	Platter, 11¾", oval	$18.00
②	Salt and pepper, pair	$22.00
⑧	Saucer	$1.00
④	Sherbet	$6.00
⑥	Sugar	$7.50
①	Tumbler	$15.00

PLATONITE

	Bowl, 4¾", berry	$3.50
	Bowl, 4¾", cream soup	$5.50
	Bowl, 8¼, large berry	$9.50
	Cup	$3.50
	Creamer	$4.50
	Plate, 6", sherbet	$1.00
	Plate, 8½", luncheon	$3.00
③	Plate, 11½", sandwich	$8.00
	Platter, 11¾", oval	$10.00
②	Salt and pepper, pair	$18.00
	Saucer	$.75
④	Sherbet	$3.50
	Sugar	$4.50
	Tumbler	$8.00

ORCHARD WARE – 1940s – 1960s
COLORS – CRYSTAL, PLATONITE AND WITH DECORATIONS AND MODERNTONE COLORS; AVOCADO GREEN

The Orchard products took several forms: apples, pears, and grapes. The most popular design was the apple. Thus, the apple design branched into several forms over time. Besides the plain crystal apple blank, there was one with an Apple Blossom design, one with a lattice look, and some Platonite versions with various applied colors or hand decorations that appeared in the 1950s. Since eating in front of the marvelous new fluttering TV screen was all the 50s rage, snack sets were a primary emphasis in this ware. Orchard ware was popular enough to span the 1940s through the 1960s.

APPLE CRYSTAL
Coaster, Cat. #818, 3", **$2.00.**
4" bowl, **$4.00.**
6" bowl, **$5.00.**
8" salad plate, **$5.00.**

THIS ALSO CAME AS A GRAPE BOWL WITH SMALL PLATES AS BOWLS, AND AS A PEAR SHAPED SALAD SET WITH PEAR-SHAPED PLATES AND SMALL BOWLS. THE SALAD FORKS AND SPOONS (PLASTIC) HAD A CROSS HATCHED DESIGN ON THE HANDLE.

APPLE WITH APPLE BLOSSOM EMBOSSING
8" snack plate with cup ring, **$5.00.**
Cup, plain or beaded handle, **$3.00.**
Saucer, **$1.00.**

APPLE LATTICE
Plate, 8", with cup ring, **$5.00.**
Cup, plain or beaded handle, **$3.00.**

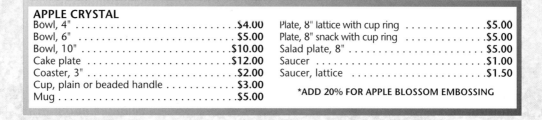

APPLE CRYSTAL

Bowl, 4" $4.00	Plate, 8" lattice with cup ring $5.00
Bowl, 6" $5.00	Plate, 8" snack with cup ring $5.00
Bowl, 10" $10.00	Salad plate, 8" $5.00
Cake plate $12.00	Saucer $1.00
Coaster, 3" $2.00	Saucer, lattice $1.50
Cup, plain or beaded handle $3.00	
Mug $5.00	***ADD 20% FOR APPLE BLOSSOM EMBOSSING**

ORCHARD WARE

APPLE MODERNTONE BOWLS
10", with blossom, **$18.00.**
without blossom, **$15.00.**

APPLE SALAD SET
With or without blossom, 10", bowl, **$15.00.**
6" bowl, assorted colors, **$8.00 each.**
10" bowl, assorted colors, **$15.00 each.**

> WE HAVE ALSO SEEN THE APPLE SALAD
> SET WITH BLACK & WHITE BOWLS.

APPLE TEA & TOAST SET
Gray and burgundy.
8" snack plate with cup ring, **$8.00 each.**
Burgundy, yellow and green,
Mugs, found with snack plates, **$5.00 each.**

APPLE MODERNTONE COLORS
Bowl, 6"	$8.00
Bowl, 10"	$15.00
Cup, plain or beaded handle	$6.00
Mug	$5.00
Plate, 8" snack with cup ring	$8.00
Salad plate, 8"	$9.00
Saucer	$2.00

*ADD 20% FOR APPLE BLOSSOM EMBOSSING

LA VISTA TEA & TOAST SET
Gray, yellow, burgundy, green.
Cup, plain or beaded handle, **$6.00 each.**
8" snack plate with cup ring, **$8.00 each.**
Set in box, **$72.00.**

APPLE DECORATED PLATONITE
Cup, plain or beaded handle, **$6.00.**
8" snack plate with cup ring, **$7.00.**

OVIDE

COLORS – GREEN, BLACK, WHITE PLATONITE TRIMMED WITH FIRED-ON COLORS IN 1950s

Varieties of decorated Ovide sets are available if you wish to start an economical collection to use.

Very little black, transparent green, or plain yellow Ovide are ever seen, but there are a few collectors asking for it. A luncheon set should be possible; but it would be simpler to put together an Ovide set in black or yellow Cloverleaf, which would be admittedly more costly but more easily found than black or yellow Ovide.

MODERNTONE
Black luncheon plate, 8", **$4.00.**
Pink cereal bowl, 5", deep, **$10.00.**
Pink saucer, **$2.00.**
Black cup, **$4.50.**

MODERNTONE
Aqua large berry bowl, 8", **$18.00.**
Aqua cup, **$4.50.**
Aqua cereal bowl, 5" deep, **$10.00.**
Burgundy flared bowl, 6", **$8.00.**

"ICE CREAM IS A CHEERFUL FOOD"
Sundaes with writing, **$16.00 each.**
Sundae liners, **$5.00 each.**

MODERNTONE BOWLS
Orange large berry bowl, 8", **$18.00.**
Orange, gray, yellow, and green,
Salad bowls, 6", **$8.00 each.**

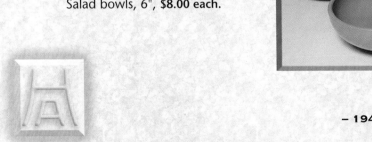

OVIDE

MODERNTONE COLORS

③	Bowl, 4¾", berry	$5.50
⑤	Creamer	$4.00
②	Cup	$4.50
①	Plate, 8", luncheon	$4.00
④	Saucer	$2.00
⑥	Sugar, open	$4.00

SET IN BOX – $90.00.

SIDE VIEW OF BREAKFAST SET BOX

BOX FOR ABOVE SET

PLATES
   Yellow, burgundy, green, gray,
      8", luncheon, **$4.00 each.**
FOOTED SUNDAES
   Gold, aqua, gray, **$8.00 each.**
SUNDAE LINERS
   Green, yellow, burgundy, gray, **$5.00 each.**

OVIDE

MODERNTONE COLORS

Ashtray, square $4.00	① Plate, 8", luncheon $4.00
Bowl, 4¾", berry $5.50	⑭ Plate, 9", dinner $8.00
⑦ Bowl, 5", cereal, deep $10.00	⑮ Platter, 11" $7.50
⑬ Bowl, 5½", shallow $6.00	④ Saucer $2.00
Bowl, 6", flared $8.00	⑥ Sugar, open $4.00
Bowl, 6", salad $8.00	Sundae, ftd. **$8.00
⑪ Bowl, 8", large berry $18.00	Sundae liner. $5.00
⑤ Creamer $4.00	⑫ Tumbler $8.00
② Cup $4.50	**Double price with advertising

OVIDE – INFORMAL

BLACK, BLUE, AND WHITE
Sugar, open, $4.50.
Dinner plate, 9", $3.50.
Cup, $3.50.
Saucer, $1.00.

BLACK, PINK, AND WHITE
Sugar, open, $4.50.
Dinner plate, 9", $3.50
Creamer, $4.50.
Cup, $3.50.
Saucer, $1.00.

BLACK, YELLOW, AND WHITE
Sugar, open, $4.50.
Creamer, $4.50.
Dinner plate, 9", $3.50.
Cup, $3.50.
Berry bowl, 4¾", $3.50.

GREEN AND YELLOW
Sugar, open, $4.50
Dinner plate, 9", $3.50.
Creamer, $4.50.

SUNRISE
Pink, yellow, and white.
Sugar, open, $4.50
Creamer, $4.50.

OVIDE
BANDS & STRIPES

BLUE AND BLACK HAIRLINE BANDS
Creamer, $4.50.
Sugar, open, $4.50.

RED AND BLACK HAIRLINE BAND
Sugar, open, $4.50.

GREEN AND BLUE BAND
Cup, $3.50.
Saucer, $1.00.

RED WIDE BAND AT TOP
Creamer, $4.50.

PLATONITE BANDS AND STRIPES

	Bowl, 4¾", berry	$3.50
⑤	Creamer	$4.50
②	Cup	$3.50
	Plate, 6", sherbet	$1.50
①	Plate, 8", luncheon	$2.50
	Plate, 9", dinner	$3.50
	Platter, 11"	$7.50
	Salt and pepper, pair	$15.00
④	Saucer	$1.00
⑰	Sherbet	$5.50
⑥	Sugar, open	$4.50
⑫	Tumbler	$12.00

OVIDE
PLATONITE WITH DESIGNS

RED BOW
Berry bowl, 4¾", **$8.00.**
Plate, 8", **$14.00.**
Cup, **$12.50.**
Saucer, **$6.00.**

RED TULIP
Creamer, **$17.50.**

RED BIRD

WINDMILLS

DESIGNS ON PLATONITE

③ Bowl, 4¾", berry	....	$8.00
⑦ Bowl, 5", cereal, deep	....	$13.00
⑪ Bowl, 8", large berry	....	$22.50
㉓ Bowl, 8", soup	....	$22.50
Candy dish and cover	....	$35.00
⑤ Creamer	....	$17.50
② Cup	....	$12.50
Cup, St. Denis	....	$12.00
① Plate, 6", sherbet	....	$6.00
Plate, 8", luncheon	....	$14.00
⑭ Plate, 9", dinner	....	$20.00
㉒ Pitcher, 16 oz.	....	$35.00
⑮ Platter, 11"	....	$22.50
Refrigerator stacking set, 4 pc.	......	$65.00
Salt and pepper, pair	....	$24.00
④ Saucer	....	$6.00
⑰ Sherbet	....	$14.00
⑥ Sugar, open	....	$17.50
⑫ Tumbler	....	$17.50

OVIDE
PLATONITE WITH DESIGNS
FLORAL

RED ASTER
    Cereal bowl, 5" deep, **$13.00.**
    Dinner plate, 9", **$20.00.**
    Cup, **$12.50.**
    Saucer, **$6.00.**

FORGET-ME-NOT – c. 1938,
Creamer, **$17.50.**

BLACK FLORAL

DESIGNS ON PLATONITE

Bowl, 4¾", berry	$8.00		Plate, 9", dinner	$20.00
⑦ Bowl, 5", cereal, deep	$13.00		Pitcher, 16 oz.	$35.00
Bowl, 8", large berry	$22.50		Platter, 11"	$22.50
Candy dish and cover	$35.00		⑳ Refrigerator stacking set, 4 pc.	$65.00
⑤ Creamer	$17.50		Salt and pepper, pair	$24.00
② Cup	$12.50		④ Saucer	$6.00
Cup, St. Denis	$12.00		⑰ Sherbet	$14.00
Plate, 6", sherbet	$6.00		Sugar, open	$17.50
Plate, 8", luncheon	$14.00		⑫ Tumbler	$17.50

OVIDE
PLATONITE WITH DESIGNS
FRUIT

PLUMS
Cup, **$12.50.**
Saucer, **$6.00.**
Luncheon plate, 8", **$14.00.**

GRAPES
Cup, **$12.50.**
Saucer, **$6.00.**
Luncheon plate, 8", **$14.00.**

APPLES
Cup, **$12.50.**
Saucer, **$6.00.**
Luncheon plate, 8", **$14.00.**

STRAWBERRIES
Cup, **$12.50.**
Saucer, **$6.00.**
Luncheon plate, 8", **$14.00.**

OVIDE
PLATONITE WITH DESIGNS
FRUIT

CUPS
   Plum, apple, grapes, strawberries, **$12.50 each.**
SAUCERS
   Plum, apple, grapes, strawberries, **$6.00 each.**

LUNCHEON PLATES, 8"
   Pear, pear & cherries, cherries, **$14.00 each.**
Without fruit
   Cup, **$3.50.**
   Saucer, **$1.00.**

CUP – ST. DENIS
   Apple design, **$12.50.**

Not shown:
   Saucer, **$6.00.**

ART DECO

NOTICE THE BLACK AND WHITE "TALL BUILDING" DESIGN IN THE DECO SET. THIS MOULDED MOTIF CAN BE FOUND IN A CRYSTAL AND GREEN FOOTED CANDY JAR, A GREEN FOOTED SALT SHAKER, AND TWO SMALL BOWLS IN GREEN. THERE IS A PLAIN AND RIBBED VERSION OF THE CEREAL BOWL. THEY ARE OBVIOUSLY VERY EARLY DESIGNS AND QUITE HARD TO LOCATE NOW. EVEN SO, THESE GREEN PIECES WILL COMMAND ONLY A TENTH OF THE PRICE OF THE ART DECO ITEMS — MORE IN LINE WITH PRICES FOR FLYING GEESE.

FLYING GEESE

ART DECO
⑤ Creamer $125.00
② Cup $100.00
① Plate, 8", luncheon $75.00
④ Saucer $25.00
⑰ Sherbet $100.00
⑥ Sugar, open $125.00
⑫ Tumbler $125.00

FLYING GEESE
③ Bowl, 4¾", berry $8.00
⑦ Bowl, 5", cereal, deep $13.00
Bowl, 8", large berry $22.50
Candy dish and cover $35.00
⑤ Creamer $17.50
Cup $12.50
Cup, St. Denis $12.00
Plate, 6", sherbet $6.00
① Plate, 8", luncheon $14.00
Plate, 9", dinner $20.00
Pitcher, 16 oz. $35.00
⑮ Platter, 11" $22.50
Refrigerator stacking set, 4 pc. $65.00
⑲ Salt and pepper, pair $24.00
Saucer $6.00
⑰ Sherbet $14.00
⑥ Sugar, open $17.50
⑫ Tumbler $17.50

OVIDE

BLACK
Sugar, **$6.50.**
Luncheon plate, 8", **$4.00.**
Bowl, 4¾", **$5.50.**
Creamer, **$6.50.**

STERLING OVERLAY
Sugar, **$10.00.**
Creamer, **$10.00.**

**BLACK DECORATION
ON PLATONITE**
Sugar, **$6.50.**
Creamer, **$6.50.**

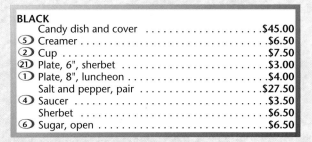

BLACK WITH STERLING

BLACK
	Candy dish and cover	$45.00
⑤	Creamer	$6.50
②	Cup	$7.50
㉑	Plate, 6", sherbet	$3.00
①	Plate, 8", luncheon	$4.00
	Salt and pepper, pair	$27.50
④	Saucer	$3.50
	Sherbet	$6.50
⑥	Sugar, open	$6.50

RIBBON
COLORS – GREEN; SOME BLACK, CRYSTAL, AND PINK

"Ribbon" is one of those hordes of 1930s wares that resonate the era in which they began, filled with unsophisticated lines and clean shapes, which manage to have elegance and movement all at the same time. "Ribbon" bowls are among the most difficult to find in all of Depression glass and their ever-increasing prices reflect that. They are in even shorter supply than those of its sister pattern, Cloverleaf.

GREEN
⑨ Bowl, 4", berry $40.00
⑦ Bowl, 5", cereal $50.00
Bowl, 8¼", large berry, flared $35.00
⑥ Bowl, 8", straight side $85.00
⑤ Candy dish and cover $65.00
⑩ Creamer, footed $13.00
② Cup $5.00
③ Plate, 6¼", sherbet $3.00
Plate, 8", luncheon $9.00
Salt and pepper, pair $30.00
Saucer $2.50
① Sherbet, footed $12.00
⑧ Sugar, footed $13.00
④ Tumbler, 6", 10 oz. $37.50
BLACK
Bowl, 8¼", large berry, flared $40.00
Plate, 8", luncheon $14.00
Salt and pepper, pr. $45.00
PINK
Salt and pepper, pair $35.00

RIPPLE

COLORS – PLATONITE WHITE AND WHITE WITH BLUE OR PINK TRIM

This Hazel-Atlas pattern had previously been known by "Crinoline," "Petticoat," "Pie Crust," and "Lasagna." A boxed set revealed the factory name. This pattern displays delightfully by mixing the colors. Be aware that the cup, creamer, and sugar handles come both plain and beaded, and that the small, shallow dessert bowl remains the most sought piece.

PLATE
Luncheon plate, 8⅞", $15.00.

CUP
Beaded handle, $5.25.
SAUCER
5⅝", $1.50.

⑧ Bowl, cereal, deep, 5⅝" $8.00
⑫ Creamer, plain or beaded handle $7.50
⑤ Cup, plain or beaded handle $3.50
① Plate, 6⅞", salad $4.00

③ Plate, 10½", sandwich $18.00
⑥ Saucer, 5⅝" $1.00
⑦ Sugar, plain or beaded handle $7.50

*DEDUCT 25% FOR UNDECORATED PLATONITE, ADD 50% FOR ALL DECORATIONS

RIPPLE

PINK

BLUE

ALL COLORS*

④ Bowl, berry, shallow, 5" $15.00

⑧ Bowl, cereal, deep, 5⅝" $8.00

⑫ Creamer, plain or beaded handle $7.50

⑤ Cup, plain or beaded handle $3.50

⑩ Mug** $6.00

① Plate, 6⅞", salad $4.00

② Plate, 8⅞", luncheon $4.00

③ Plate, 10½", sandwich $18.00

⑥ Saucer, 5⅝" $1.00

⑦ Sugar, plain or beaded handle $7.50

⑨ Tidbit, 3-tier $35.00

⑪ Tumbler, 5", 12 oz.** $8.00

*DEDUCT 25% FOR UNDECORATED PLATONITE **FOUND PACKED IN SOME SETS
ADD 50% FOR DECORATIONS

ROXANA

COLORS – "GOLDEN TOPAZ," CRYSTAL, AND SOME PLATONITE

Roxana was only chronicled by Hazel-Atlas for one year. It is truly a limited pattern when compared to the thousands of pieces made in other patterns over the years. Only the 4½" deep bowl has been found in Platonite.

YELLOW
- ⑤ Bowl, 4½" x 2⅜" $15.00
- ② Bowl, 5", berry $16.00
- ⑦ Bowl, 6", cereal $22.00
- ④ Plate, 5½" $12.00
- ③ Plate, 6", sherbet $10.00
- ⑥ Sherbet, footed $12.00
- ① Tumbler, 4¼", 9 oz. $25.00

PLATONITE
- Bowl, 4½" x 2⅜" $20.00

ONE OF THESE PIECES OF
GOLDEN TOPAZ
GLASSWARE
IN EVERY PACKAGE

The cost of the ware is included in the price of the package and we hereby authorize your grocer to show it to you

STAR A STAR
BRAND

NEW PROCESS
OATS
WITH GOLDEN TOPAZ
TABLE GLASSWARE
PACKED FOR
SYMONS BROS. & CO.
SAGINAW, JACKSON, ALMA

FRONT OF STAR BRAND OATS BOX.

ROYAL LACE
COLORS – COBALT BLUE, CRYSTAL, GREEN, PINK; SOME AMETHYST

Royal Lace collectors searching for green number almost as many as for the lovely cobalt blue. Green is found in quantity in England. The 4⅞", 10-ounce tumblers have all been swallowed up into collections; but the number of iced teas and juice tumblers is rapidly diminishing. Both a rolled-edge console bowl and rolled-edge candlesticks have been found in amethyst Royal Lace. The only other amethyst pieces are the sherbets in metal holders and the cookie jar bottom used for toddy sets.

BLUE

Bowl, 4¾", cream soup	$50.00
Bowl, 5", berry	$75.00
Bowl, 10", round berry	$85.00
Bowl, 10", 3-legged, straight edge	$95.00
Bowl, 10", 3-legged rolled edge	$650.00
Bowl, 10", 3-legged, ruffled edge	$750.00
Bowl, 11", oval vegetable	$75.00
Butter dish and cover	$695.00
Butter dish bottom	$495.00
Butter dish top	$200.00
Candlestick, straight edge, pair	$165.00
Candlestick, rolled edge, pair	$550.00
Candlestick, ruffled edge, pair	$575.00

① Cookie jar and cover	$385.00
④ Cream, footed	$60.00
Cup	$45.00
Nut bowl	$1,695.00
Pitcher, 48 oz., straight sides	$190.00
Pitcher, 64 oz., 8", without lip	$295.00
Pitcher, 8", 68 oz., with lip	$295.00
Pitcher, 8", 86 oz., without lip	$325.00
Pitcher, 8½", 96 oz., with lip	$525.00
Plate, 6", sherbet	$17.00
Plate, 8½", luncheon	$43.00
㉒ Plate, 9⅞", dinner	$48.00
Plate, 9⅞", grill	$40.00
Platter, 13", oval	$70.00

⑬ Salt and pepper, pair	$340.00
Saucer	$12.00
Sherbet, footed	$60.00
㉑ Sherbet in metal holder	$42.00
⑤ Sugar	$40.00
⑩ Sugar lid	$195.00
Tumbler, 3½", 5 oz.	$60.00
Tumbler, 4⅛", 9 oz.	$53.00
Tumbler, 4⅞", 10 oz.	$165.00
Tumbler, 5⅜", 12 oz.	$132.00
Toddy or cider set	$295.00

(includes cookie jar, metal lid, metal tray,
8 roly-poly cups, and ladle)

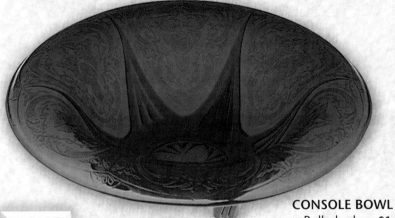

AMETHYST

Bowl, 10", 3-legged rolled edge	$1,000.00
Candlestick, rolled edge, pair	$1,000.00
Sherbet in metal holder	$40.00
Toddy or cider set	$295.00

(includes cookie jar, metal lid, metal tray, 8 roly-poly cups, and ladle)

CONSOLE BOWL
Rolled edge, **$1,000.00.**

ROYAL LACE

CRYSTAL

Bowl, 4¾", cream soup $17.50
Bowl, 5", berry $18.00
Bowl, 10", round berry $20.00
Bowl, 10", 3-legged, straight edge $35.00
Bowl, 10", 3-legged rolled edge .$295.00
Bowl, 10", 3-legged, ruffled edge $55.00
Bowl, 11", oval vegetable $28.00
Butter dish and cover $80.00
Butter dish bottom $50.00
Butter dish top $30.00
Candlestick, straight edge, pair . .$40.00
Candlestick, rolled edge, pair $60.00
Candlestick, ruffled edge, pair $50.00

① Cookie jar and cover $35.00
④ Cream, footed $16.00
   Cup $9.00
   Nut bowl $500.00
   Pitcher, 48 oz., straight sides $40.00
   Pitcher, 64 oz., 8", without lip . . $45.00
⑦ Pitcher, 8", 68 oz., with lip $50.00
   Pitcher, 8", 86 oz., without lip . .$50.00
   Pitcher, 8½", 96 oz., with lip $75.00
   Plate, 6", sherbet $8.00
   Plate, 8½", luncheon $8.00
   Plate, 9⅞", dinner $18.00
⑥ Plate, 9⅞", grill $11.00

③ Platter, 13", oval $20.00
   Salt and pepper, pair $42.00
   Saucer $5.00
   Sherbet, footed $17.00
   Sherbet in metal holder $4.00
⑤ Sugar $11.00
⑩ Sugar lid $20.00
⑧ Tumbler, 3½", 5 oz. $20.00
② Tumbler, 4⅛", 9 oz. $16.00
   Tumbler, 4⅞", 10 oz. $40.00
⑨ Tumbler, 5⅜", 12 oz. $40.00

IRIDESCENT
Sugar, $50.00.

ROYAL LACE

GREEN

⑱ Bowl, 4¾", cream soup	$38.00
Bowl, 5", berry	$38.00
⑮ Bowl, 10", round berry	$30.00
Bowl, 10", 3-legged, straight edge	$75.00
Bowl, 10", 3-legged rolled edge	$145.00
Bowl, 10", 3-legged, ruffled edge	$135.00
Bowl, 11", oval vegetable	$45.00
Butter dish and cover	$275.00
Butter dish bottom	$180.00
Butter dish top	$95.00
Candlestick, straight edge, pair	$95.00
Candlestick, rolled edge, pair	$175.00
Candlestick, ruffled edge, pair	$195.00

Cookie jar and cover	$100.00
④ Cream, footed	$28.00
⑲ Cup	$20.00
Nut bowl, 5"	$650.00
Pitcher, 48 oz., straight sides	$135.00
Pitcher, 64 oz., 8", without lip	$120.00
Pitcher, 8", 68 oz., with lip	$225.00
Pitcher, 8", 86 oz., without lip	$175.00
Pitcher, 8½", 96 oz., with lip	$160.00
Plate, 6", sherbet	$12.00
Plate, 8½", luncheon	$16.00
Plate, 9⅞", dinner	$38.00
Plate, 9⅞", grill	$28.00

③ Platter, 13", oval	$42.00
⑬ Salt and pepper, pair	$140.00
⑳ Saucer	$10.00
⑪ Sherbet, footed	$25.00
⑤ Sugar	$22.00
Sugar lid	$60.00
Tumbler, 3½", 5 oz.	$40.00
Tumbler, 4⅛", 9 oz.	$32.00
Tumbler, 4⅞", 10 oz.	$95.00
Tumbler, 5⅜", 12 oz.	$75.00

NUT BOWL
Green, 5", $650.00.

ROYAL LACE

PINK

Bowl, 4¾", cream soup $32.00	Cookie jar and cover $60.00	Platter, 13", oval $45.00
⑫ Bowl, 5", berry $35.00	Cream, footed $22.00	⑬ Salt and pepper, pair $65.00
⑮ Bowl, 10", round berry $40.00	Cup $22.00	Saucer $7.00
⑯ Bowl, 10", 3-legged, straight edge $65.00	Nut bowl, 5" $650.00	⑪ Sherbet, footed $20.00
㉓ Bowl, 10", 3-legged rolled edge .$120.00	Pitcher, 48 oz., straight sides . . .$100.00	Sugar $20.00
Bowl, 10", 3-legged, ruffled edge $125.00	Pitcher, 64 oz., 8", without lip . .$110.00	Sugar lid $60.00
Bowl, 11", oval vegetable $40.00	Pitcher, 8", 68 oz., with lip $115.00	Tumbler, 3½", 5 oz. $33.00
⑰ Butter dish and cover $195.00	Pitcher, 8", 86 oz., without lip . .$135.00	② Tumbler, 4⅛", 9 oz. $28.00
Butter dish bottom $140.00	⑭ Pitcher, 8½", 96 oz., with lip . . .$150.00	Tumbler, 4⅞", 10 oz. $85.00
Butter dish top $55.00	Plate, 6", sherbet $9.00	⑨ Tumbler, 5⅜", 12 oz. $75.00
Candlestick, straight edge, pair . . .$75.00	Plate, 8½", luncheon $15.00	
Candlestick, rolled edge, pair . . .$155.00	Plate, 9⅞", dinner $33.00	
Candlestick, ruffled edge, pair . . .$150.00	Plate, 9⅞", grill $22.00	

NUT BOWL
Pink, 5", $650.00.

"SHIPS"/"WHITE SHIPS"

COLORS – COBALT BLUE WITH WHITE, YELLOW, AND RED DECORATION, CRYSTAL WITH BLUE

Cobalt Moderntone decorated with white "Ships" is now rarely seen, especially in mint condition. Sherbet plates are harder to find than dinner plates, but both have vanished into long-standing collections. At least one yellow "Ships" old-fashioned tumbler has surfaced in "raincoat" yellow. Pieces are found with red and white "Ships" on crystal tumblers with a blue boat.

"SHIPS"

① Cup (plain), "Moderntone"	....	$11.00
Cocktail mixer with stirrer	....	$35.00
Cocktail shaker	....	$50.00
Ice bowl	....	$40.00
⑤ Pitcher without lip, 82 oz.	....	$65.00
Pitcher with lip, 86 oz.	....	$75.00
⑩ Plate, 5⅞", sherbet	....	$36.00
⑦ Plate, 8", salad	....	$46.00
② Plate, 9", dinner	....	$56.00
③ Saucer	....	$26.00
⑨ Tumbler, 2 oz., 2¼", shot glass	....	$235.00
Tumbler, 4 oz., 3¼", heavy bottom	....	$28.00
Tumbler, 5 oz., 3¾", juice	....	$15.00
⑥ Tumbler, 6 oz., roly poly	....	$15.00
Tumbler, 8 oz., 3⅜", old fashioned	....	$20.00
Tumbler, 9 oz., 3¾", straight, water	....	$15.00
④ Tumbler, 9 oz., 4⅝", water	....	$12.00
Tumbler, 10½ oz., 4⅞", iced tea	....	$16.00
⑧ Tumbler, 12 oz., iced tea	....	$15.00
Tumbler, 15 oz., large tea	....	$40.00

PITCHER
Concentric Rings
With lip, 86 oz., **$75.00.**

SIMPLICITY – 1960s

Hazel Ware Simplicity was made in the 60s on Colony Square blanks; but it was called Simplicity when issued in crystal. There is a possibility of other pieces like any of those found in Moroccan Amethyst or Capri color listed in the patterns mentioned.

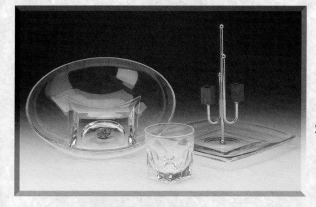

SIMPLICITY
Bowl, 10¾", $10.00.
Tumbler, 3¹⁄₁₆", $3.00.
Candleholder, 8", $12.00.

CRYSTAL
Bowl, 6"	$4.00
Bowl, 10¾"	$10.00
Candleholder, 8"	$12.00
Cup, Colony Square	$2.00
Plate, 8", Colony Square	$5.00
Saucer	$.50
Tumbler, 3¹⁄₁₆"	$3.00
Tumbler, 4¼"	$4.00

"SQUARE DECORATED GAY FAD STUDIOS" – 1950s

HAWAIIAN FLOWERS – Coral Frangipane lunch set.

WHITE CEREUS/YELLOW HIBISCUS – Lunch sets.

ROSEMAILING
Tea & toast set.

IVY
Lunch set.

RED ANTHURIUM
Tea & toast set.

YELLOW HIBISCUS & CORAL FRANGIPANE
Luncheon sets.
WHITE CEREUS
Tea & toast sets.

NOTICE THE TOAST PLATES COME WITH RINGS FOR CUPS.

NOT SHOWN, BUT SEEN FOR SALE, IS CRYSTAL SQAURE WITH A FROSTED PINK TRIM ON PLATE EDGES AND CUP HANDLES.

Cup	$6.00
Plate, 8"	$8.00
Plate, luncheon or toast with ring, 8"	$8.00
Saucer	$2.00

STARLIGHT

COLORS – CRYSTAL, PINK; SOME PLATONITE, COBALT

Starlight is an economically priced pattern; the difficulty is locating it. This small pattern has never been assembled by large numbers of collectors, but the ones who do try for a set report shortages of sherbets, cereals, and the large salad bowls and liner/serving plates. Pink and cobalt blue bowls make nice accessory pieces with the crystal, but only bowls are available in these colors.

PLATONITE
Dinner plate, 9", **$8.00.**
Cup, **$5.00.**
Saucer, **$2.00.**

BOWLS
8½", closed handles.
Pink, **$20.00.**
Cobalt, **$35.00.**

CRYSTAL

CRYSTAL/PLATONITE
⑦ Bowl, 5½", cereal, closed handles . **$8.00**
   Bowl, 8½", closed handles **$12.00**
⑧ Bowl, 11½", salad **$30.00**
   Bowl, 12", 2¾" deep **$40.00**
⑥ Creamer, oval **$8.00**
② Cup **$5.00**
⑩ Plate, 6", bread and butter **$3.00**
   Plate, 8½", luncheon **$5.00**
① Plate, 9", dinner **$8.00**
⑨ Plate, 13", sandwich **$15.00**

⑬ Relish dish **$15.00**
⑪ Salt and pepper, pair **$22.50**
③ Saucer **$2.00**
⑫ Sherbet **$15.00**
⑤ Sugar, oval **$8.00**
PINK
   Bowl, 5½", cereal, closed handles **$12.00**
   Bowl, 8½", closed handles **$20.00**
   Plate, 13", sandwich **$18.00**
COBALT
   Bowl, 8½", closed handles **$35.00**

VOGUE – MID-1950s

COLORS – CRYSTAL AND WITH DECORATIONS

Vogue was advertised as ware "in the Swedish manner" with a heavy sham base; and since Swedish modern furniture was taking the country by storm in the 1950s, it makes sense that glassware would follow the trend of the time.

CHIP AND DIP
Grapes with metal hanger, **$18.00.**

VOGUE BLANK
With large convex dots, known as "El Dorado," c. 1970s.
Avocado green, Granada gold, candy with lid, **$12.50 each.**

OTHER ITEMS ARE AVAILABLE IN THE LATER DESIGNS.

CANDY DISH
7"h with lid, c. 1955, **$12.00.**

OTHERS HAVE BEEN FOUND WITH THIS BLUE LEAF DESIGN

Bowl, 4¾"	$5.00
Bowl, 9", salad	$8.00
Candy with lid, 7"	$12.00
Chip and dip with metal hanger	$15.00
Pitcher, 64 oz.	$12.00
Salad, large bowl, 9"	$8.00
Salad, small bowl, 4¾"	$5.00
Tumbler, 6 oz. juice	$3.00
Tumbler, 8 oz. rocks	$4.00
Tumbler, 12 oz. beverage	$5.00
Tumbler, 16 oz. cooler	$6.00
Tumbler, 25 oz. tea	$8.00

WILLOW – 1940s – 1950s

COLORS – CRYSTAL WITH BLUE OR RED; FROSTED CRYSTAL WITH BLUE OR RED; PLATONITE WITH BLUE OR RED

PLATONITE WITH BLUE
    Tumbler, 4 oz., 3", $10.00.
    Tumbler, 12 oz., 5", $15.00.
    Cottage cheese bowl, 5", $12.50.

FROSTED CRYSTAL WITH BLUE
    Frosted glass, plastic lids. Both marked HA.
    Syrup pitcher, 6"h, $50.00.
    Batter pitcher, pancake, 9"h, $75.00.
Courtesy of Mary Frank Gaston,
Blue Willow: Identification and Value Guide, Revised 2nd Edition.

CRYSTAL WITH BLUE
    Cocktail shaker, $75.00.
    Matching tumblers, 4 oz., 3", **$10.00 each.**

Batter pitcher, pancake, 9"h	$75.00
Bowl, cottage cheese, 5"	$12.50
Cocktail shaker	$75.00
Pitcher, 80 oz.	$95.00
Syrup pitcher, 6"h	$50.00
Tumbler, 4 oz., 3"	$10.00
Tumbler, 9 oz., 4"	$12.00
Tumbler, 12 oz., 5"	$15.00

X-DESIGN – 1930s

COLORS – GREEN, PINK

Possibly there are other items to be found in this design. These are the ones we have found.

BOWL
7", $22.00.

CANDY DISH
With lid, $35.00.

CREAMER – $18.00.
SHAKERS – $45.00 pair.

Bowl, 4"	$10.00
Bowl, 7"	$22.00
Butter dish with cover	$35.00
Candy dish with lid	$35.00
Creamer	$18.00
Shaker, pr.	$45.00
Sugar	$12.00
Sugar lid	$15.00

BIBLIOGRAPHY

Algeo, J.S. *The Story of Hazel-Atlas Glass Company.* Unpublished. 1956.

Butler Bros. *Wholesale Catalogue,* 1927.

Charge into '70 with Hazelware.... Continental Can Company.

Chase, Mark & Michael Kelly. *Collectible Drinking Glasses, Identification and Values.* Collector Books, 1996.

Florence, Gene. *Florences' Glass Kitchen Shakers, 1930 - 1950s.* Collector Books, 2004.

————————. *Kitchen Glassware of the Depression Years, Identification & Values.* Collector Books, 2003.

————————. *Treasures of Very Rare Depression Glass, Identification and Value Guide.* Collectors Books, 2003.

Florence, Gene and Cathy. *Collector's Encyclopedia of Depression Glass.* Collector Books, 2004.

————————. *Collectible Glassware from the 40s, 50s, & 60s,* 5th ed. Collector Books, 2004.

Glassware by Hazel-Atlas. Continental Can Company, 1957.

Glassware by Hazel-Atlas. Hazel-Atlas Glass Company, 1955.

Hazelware Florist Catalogue 1970. Continental Can Company Brochure, 1970.

Louisville Tin & Stove Co., Inc., Catalogue, 1937

Mirken, Alan. ed. *1927 Edition of The Sears, Roebuck Catalogue, The Roaring Twenties.* Crown Publishers, Inc. 1970.

Six, Dean. *West Virginia Glass Between the Wars.* Schiffer Publishing, Ltd., 2002.

Six, Dean, ed. F.O.B. Clarksburg, W.Va. *Hazel Atlas Glass After the Depression Era.* West Virginia Museum of American Glass, Ltd. 2002.

Stout, Sandra McPhee. *Depression Glass Number Two.* Wallace-Homestead Books, 1971.

Visakay, Stephen. *Vintage Bar Ware, Identification and Value Guide.* Collector Books, 1997.

Weatherman, Hazel Marie. *Colored Glassware of the Depression Era, 2.* Hazelglass books, 1974.

————————. *The Decorated Tumbler.* Glassbooks, Inc., 1978.

NOTE FROM AUTHOR:

It would be a wonderful help to those actively looking for marked Hazel-Atlas objects if you would refrain from putting price tags over the company marks on the bottoms of pieces. We've done it, but it feels very uncomfortable peeling up bottom labels to see what company mark is shown there — if there is one!

Gene M. Florence, Jr., a native Kentuckian, graduated from the University of Kentucky in 1967. He held a double major in mathematics and English that he immediately put to use in industry and subsequently, in teaching junior and senior high school.

A collector since childhood, Mr. Florence progressed from baseball cards, comic books, coins, and bottles to glassware. His buying and selling glassware "hobby" began to override his nine-year teaching career. In the summer of 1972, he wrote a book on Depression glassware that was well received by collectors in the field, persuading him to leave teaching in 1976 and pursue the antique glass business full time. This allowed time to travel to glass shows throughout the country, where he assiduously studied the prices of glass being sold... and of that remaining unsold.

Cathy Gaines Florence, also a native Kentuckian, graduated with honors and a coveted voice award from high school, attended Georgetown College where she obtained a French major and an English minor, then married her middle-school sweetheart Gene Florence.

She taught four years at the middle school level, then worked part-time while raising two boys. It was then that she typed her husband's first manuscript, written in "chicken scratch." The first three or four letters of each word would be legible and then it was up to her to guess what the last was. To their astonishment, the book sold well and a new career was born for her husband and their lives took different turns from the teaching careers they'd planned.

In the mid-80s she authored a book on collecting quilts, harking back to skills taught her by her grandmothers; and she has since co-authored books on glass with husband Gene.

Books written by the Florences include the following titles: *The Collector's Encyclopedia of Depression Glass, Stemware Identification, The Collector's Encyclopedia of Akro Agate, Pocket Guide to Depression Glass & More, Kitchen Glassware of the Depression Years, Collectible Glassware from the 40s, 50s, and 60s, Glass Candlesticks of the Depression Era, Anchor Hocking's Fire-King & More, Florences' Glassware Pattern Identification Guide, Florence's Big Book of Salt and Pepper Shakers, Standard Baseball Card Price Guide,* six editions of *Very Rare Glassware of the Depression Years,* and *Treasures of Very Rare Depression Glass.* Gene has also written six volumes of *The Collector's Encyclopedia of Occupied Japan* and a book on Degenhart glassware for that museum. Mr. and Mrs. Florence's most recent books are *Florences' Glass Kitchen Shakers, 1930 – 1950s* and *The Hazel-Atlas Glass Identification and Value Guide.*

OTHER BOOKS BY GENE & CATHY FLORENCE

ELEGANT GLASSWARE, OF THE DEPRESSION ERA, ELEVENTH EDITION
Gene & Cathy Florence

This eleventh edition holds more than 100 new photographs, listings, and updated values. Featured is the handmade and acid-etched glassware that was sold in department and jewelry stores from the Depression era through the 1950s, not the dimestore and giveaway items known as Depression glass. Large group settings are included for each of the more than 100 patterns, as well as close-ups to show pattern details. For the first time all pieces in photographs are identified and cross-referenced with their listings. The famous glassmakers presented include Fenton, Cambridge, Heisey, Tiffin, Imperial, Duncan & Miller, U.S. Glass, and Paden City.

Item #6327 • ISBN: 1-57432-353-9 • 8½ x 11 • 256 Pgs. • HB • $19.95

POCKET GUIDE TO DEPRESSION GLASS & MORE, FOURTEENTH EDITION
Gene & Cathy Florence

Gene and Cathy Florenece have completely revised their Pocket Guide to Depression Glass and More, with over 4,000 values updated to reflect the ever-changing market. There are a total of 47 new photos for this edition. These gorgeous photographs show great detail, and the listings of the patterns and their available pieces make identification simple. For the first time all pieces in photographs are identified and cross-referenced with their listings. There is even a section on re-issues and the numerous fakes flooding the market.

Item #6556 • ISBN: 1-57432-414-4 • 5½ x 8½ • 224 Pgs • PB • $12.95

COLLECTOR'S ENCYCLOPEDIA OF DEPRESSION GLASS, SIXTEENTH EDITION
Gene & Cathy Florence

Since its first edition in 1972, this book has been America's #1 bestselling glass book. This completely revised sixteenth edition features the previous 133 patterns plus 11 additional patterns, to make this the most complete reference to date. Dealing primarily with the glass made from the 1920s through the end of the 1930s, this beautiful reference book contains stunning color photographs, vintage catalog pages, 2004 values, and a special section on reissues and fakes.

Item #6327 • ISBN: 1-57432-353-9 • 8½ x 11 • 256 Pgs. • HB • $19.95

TREASURES OF VERY RARE DEPRESSION GLASS
Gene Florence

This book features over 1,000 rare or sometimes one-of-a-kind examples of Depression items, as well as elegant and kitchen items. Glass companies featured include Duncan & Miller, Federal, Fostoria, Fenton, A.H. Heisey, Hocking, Imperial, Jeannette, Paden City, Tiffin, and more. 2003 values.

Item #6241 • ISBN: 1-57432-336-9 • 8½ x 11 • 368 Pgs. • HB • $39.95

FLORENCES' GLASS KITCHEN SHAKERS, 1930 – 1950s
Gene & Cathy Florence

Over 1,000 glass kitchen shakers, including sugar shakers, are pictured in this volume of full-color group photographs. Catalog identification of previously unknown shaker names is provided, as well as name, company, and value given for each item shown. Companies featured include Hazel-Atlas, Anchor Hocking, Jeannette, McKee, Owens-Illinois, and Tipp City Decorations. 2004 values.

Item #6462 • ISBN: 1-57432-389-X • 8½ x 11 • 160 Pgs • PB • $19.95

FLORENCES' BIG BOOK OF SALT & PEPPER SHAKERS
Gene & Cathy Florence

Over 5,000 shakers photographed in full color are featured. Categories include advertising products, animals, chefs, Christmas, decorative, domestic items, ethnic groups, famous characters, gambling, garden items, glass, heads, lamps and lighting, metal, miniature, musical, nodders, Occupied Japan, odd pairs, plastic/celluloid, pottery, religious, risqué, singles, souvenir, sports, steins, transportation, Western themes, wood, and World's Fairs. Famous potteries are represented — Lefton, Holt Howard, Vandor, Shawnee, and more. This book also includes examples of the highly prized Depression glass shakers. 2005 values.

Item #5918 • ISBN: 1-57432-257-5 • 8½ x 11 • 272 Pgs. • PB • $24.95

COLLECTIBLE GLASSWARE FROM THE 40s, 50s & 60s, SEVENTH EDITION

Gene & Cathy Florence

Covering post-Depression era collectible glassware, this is the only book available that deals exclusively with the handmade and mass-produced glassware from the 40s, 50s, and 60s. It is completely updated, featuring many original company catalog pages and 19 new patterns — making a total of 121 patterns from Anniversary to Yorktown, with many of the most popular Fire-King patterns in between. 2004 values.

Item #6325 • ISBN: 1-57432-351-2 • 8½ x 11 • 256 Pgs. • HB • $19.95

ANCHOR HOCKING'S FIRE-KING & MORE, SECOND EDITION

Gene Florence

From the 1930s to the 1960s Anchor Hocking Glass Corp. of Lancaster, Ohio, produced an extensive line of glassware called Fire-King. Their lines included not only dinnerware but also a plethora of glass kitchen items — reamers, measuring cups, mixing bowls, mugs, and more. This is the essential collectors' reference to this massive line of glassware. It's loaded with hundreds of new full-color photos, vintage catalog pages, company materials, facts, information, and values. 2005 values.

Item #5602 • ISBN: 1-57432-164-1 • 8½ x 11 • 224 Pgs. • HB • $24.95

GLASS CANDLESTICKS OF THE DEPRESSION ERA

Gene Florence

More than 500 different candlesticks are shown in this book in full-color photographs. The book is arranged according to color: amber, black, blue, crystal, green, iridescent, multicolor, pink, purple, red, smoke, white, and yellow. Many famous glassmakers are represented, such as Heisey, Cambridge, Fostoria, and Tiffin. The descriptive text for each candleholder includes pattern, maker, color, height, and current collector value. A helpful index and bibliography are also provided. 2000 values.

Item #5354 • ISBN: 1-57432-136-6 • 8½ x 11 • 176 Pgs. • HB • $24.95

KITCHEN GLASSWARE OF THE DEPRESSION YEARS, SIXTH EDITION

Gene & Cathy Florence

More than 5,000 items are showcased in beautiful professional color photographs with descriptions and values. The highly collectible glass from the Depression era through the 1960s fills its pages, in addition to the ever-popular Fire-King and Pyrex glassware. This comprehensive encyclopedia provides an easy-to-use format, showing items by color, shape, or pattern. 2005 values.

Item #5827 • ISBN: 1-57432-220-6 • 8½ x 11 • 272 Pgs. • HB • $24.95

FLORENCES' GLASSWARE PATTERN IDENTIFICATION GUIDES

Gene & Cathy Florence

Florences' Glassware Pattern Identification Guides are great companions for the Florences' other glassware books. Volume I includes every pattern featured in *Collector's Encyclopedia of Depression Glass, Collectible Glassware from the 40s, 50s, and 60s,* and *Elegant Glassware of the Depression Era,* as well as many more — nearly 400 patterns in all. Volume II holds nearly 500 patterns, with no repeats from Volume I. Volume III also showcases nearly 500 patterns with no repeats from the previous volumes. Carefully planned close-up photographs of representative pieces for every pattern show great detail to make identification easy. With every pattern, the Florences provide the names, the companies that made the glass, dates of production, and even colors available. No values.

Vol. I • Item #5042 • ISBN: 1-57432-045-9 • 8½ x 11 • 176 Pgs. • PB • $18.95
Vol. II • Item #5615 • ISBN: 1-57432-177-3 • 8½ x 11 • 208 Pgs. • PB • $19.95
Vol. III • Item #6142 • ISBN: 1-57432-315-6 • 8½ x 11 • 272 Pgs. • PB • $19.95

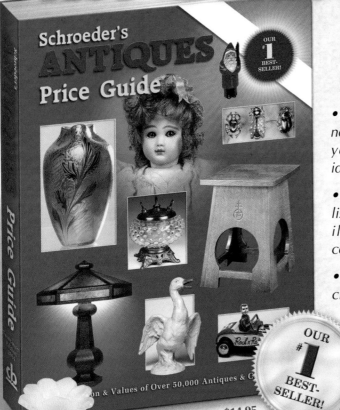